THE

THEOGONY

OF THE

HINDOOS

THE THEOGONY OF THE HINDOOS;

WITH THEIR SYSTEMS OF

PHILOSOPHY AND COSMOGONY.

An Essay.

BY

COUNT M. BJÖRNSTJERNA

GYAN

Published by

GYAN

Gyan Publishing House
5, Ansari Road
Daryaganj, New Delhi-110002
Phone: 011-47034999, 9811692060
E-mail: books@gyanbooks.com

Distribution Network
gyanbooks.com
India, USA, Canada, UK, Australia, France

ISBN: 978-81-212-8118-8 (PB)
First Published, 1844

2nd Impression 2023

Printed at: Gyan Press, Delhi.

THE THEOGONY OF THE HINDOOS
Author: COUNT M. BJÖRNSTJERNA

THE THEOGONY OF THE HINDOOS;

WITH THEIR SYSTEMS OF

PHILOSOPHY AND COSMOGONY.

An Essay.

BY

COUNT M. BJÖRNSTJERNA,

AUTHOR OF 'THE BRITISH EMPIRE IN THE EAST.'

LONDON:

JOHN MURRAY, ALBEMARLE STREET.

1844.

ADVERTISEMENT.

THE Essay which we here put into the hands of the public was originally written in the *Swedish* language, being the Author's native tongue. It is now about two years since it was first published at Stockholm.

We here present it in an English translation, revised by the author himself, with various corrections and improvements. We are happy to say that the translation has met with the approbation of the author; whilst the additions to the original give it rather the character of a new and revised work, than that of a mere English version of the original edition.

Should the present essay meet with as favourable a reception as that of its predecessor,* we shall feel ourselves amply rewarded in the consciousness that our labour has not been in vain.

* 'The British Empire in the East.'

TABLE OF CONTENTS.

THE RELIGION OF THE HINDOOS.

PHILOSOPHIC SYSTEMS OF THE HINDOOS.

THE EPIC POETRY OF THE HINDOOS, AS A PART OF THEIR RELIGION.

BUDDHISM.

THE JAINAS.

THE SHEIKS.

THE MAHOMETAN TRIBES IN INDIA, THE GUEBERS OR PARSES, AND THE SYRIAN CHRISTIANS IN INDIA.

THE COSMOGONY OF THE HINDOOS COMPARED WITH THE COSMOGONIES OF THE OTHER MOST ANCIENT NATIONS.

OF THE FIRST MIGRATION OF NATIONS ON THE EARTH.

INTRODUCTION.

Herodotus, the father of classic history, relates, that after *Cyrus* had conquered the greater part of Asia, and his successor, *Darius Hystaspes*, had continued these conquests, the northern point of *Hindostan* (the present *Punjab*) formed one of the twenty-four provinces which constituted the kingdom of *Darius*. About one hundred and sixty years after this king's death, *Alexander* commenced his expedition against India, probably because it had discontinued paying the tribute imposed by the former. From *Sogdiana* (the present *Sumarcand*), and from *Bactria* (*Balkh*), the Grecian conqueror conducted his army over the *Paropamian* chain of mountains, now called *Hindu-Kosh*,* to *India*, which was then the object of his ambition (*vide* Strabo and Arrian).

* Alexander built a city on the southern side of this chain of mountains, which bore his name (Arrian, iv.) and is probably the present *Cabul*.

At the river *Hyphasis*,* Alexander fell in with *Agrames,* king of the *Gangarides*,† who, with 20,000 cavalry, 100,000 infantry, and 2000 war chariots,‡ stopped the way of the hitherto unrestrained conqueror. An insurrection broke out in Alexander's army, which compelled him to return to the *Hydaspes.* Here he built vessels, embarked a part of his army, followed the stream downwards as far as its conjunction with the *Indus,* and proceeded on this river down to *Patula,* the present *Tatah,* from which place he returned by the Persian Gulf, to the conquered provinces on the *Tigris* and the *Euphrates.*

The resistance made by the Indian kings, the great number of their forces, the multitude of their war chariots, the excellence of their arms, and the strength of their fortresses, prove what India was even at that time.§

* This river is now called *Beeja,* which, after its conjunction with *Hesudrus* (now *Sutledge*), falls into the *Hydaspes* (now *Jellum*), and together with the latter into the *Indus.*

† The countries about the *Ganges*, probably the most northern parts of the same, *Rohilcund*, *Oude*, and *Bareilly.*

‡ Vide Arrian and Quintus Curtius, Lib. ix. Cap. 11.

§ More than 1200 years earlier, another conqueror (*Krischna*) had victoriously marched through India, surrounded by dancing *Bacchantes* crowned with vine-branches. It is this

The earliest writers, after *Herodotus*, who have given any information to Europe respecting India, are *Arrian* and *Diodorus*. Their accounts originate for the greater part from *Megasthenes*, who was sent by Alexander as ambassador to the king of the *Prasians*, whose capital was *Palibothra*, now *Patna*,* in the province of *Bahar*. Megasthenes relates that there were then 118 independent kingdoms in India, and that *Palibothra* was two geographical miles† in length, and one mile in breadth, and was surrounded by a wall with 570 towers, and 64 gates.‡ He also mentions the high degree of culture which India had already attained; that the land was full of large and rich cities, had a considerable trade, and roads in all directions, with mile-stones, and was provided with inns for travellers.

Strabo, *Plutarch*, and *Apollodorus* agree in these statements. *Strabo* makes mention of the wealth which prevailed in India, how the

historic fact, which is celebrated in the famous sanscrit poem *Mâhab-hârata*, that has given rise to the *mythological* narrative of the Greeks respecting the procession of *Bacchus* to India.

* Vide Rennel's Geographical System of Herodotus.

† 15 to a degree.

‡ Strabo, Lib. xv.

elephants were covered with gold and silver ornaments, the drinking vessels set with precious stones, and the people of rank clothed in gold brocade adorned with pearls. *Aristobulus* mentions the chastity of the Hindoo wife, and her voluntary death by burning, on the decease of her husband, as is the case at the present day.

A long period elapsed after the Greeks before any further information was obtained respecting this country. *St. Clemens* and *St. Ambrose* were the only authors of the middle ages who have given any accounts of it, and of so uncertain a character, that little reliance can be placed upon them.

After these fathers of the church, *Ibn-Batuta,* a native of Morocco, from *Tangiers,* has given the most correct information. He undertook a journey to the east in the year 1324, which continued till 1353, twenty-nine years. *Batuta* visited Algiers, Tunis, Tripoli, Egypt, Syria, Arabia, Persia, Khorassan, Afghanistan, India twice, Tibet, China, Sumatra and Java, and returned by Ormus, Shiraz, Ispahan, Aleppo, Mecca, Jerusalem and Gibraltar, to Morocco, an astonishing journey for this period.

During his stay in India, *Batuta* gained the favour of *Muhammed*, the emperor of Delhi, who despatched him with an embassy to the emperor of China. This Muhammed was a descendant of the sultans of Khorassan, who had conquered a part of India, all of whom took the surname of *Oddin*, or *Ud-din*.

Batuta's retinue consisted of no less than 1000 persons. He set out from Delhi in the year 1342, and took with him presents, which show what splendor and opulence prevailed at the court of Delhi. These consisted of 100 Arabian horses, richly bridled and saddled; 100 Bayaderes, distinguished for their beauty; five dresses worked with jewels; 500 dresses of gold and silk; 1000 dresses of various kinds of materials, together with a great number of vessels of gold, swords with jewels, &c.*

The description of the manifold disasters of the embassy is interesting; in other respects *Batuta's* account is nothing but a statement of the names of the places which he visited. It is written in Arabic, and has been translated

* The embassy was plundered on the way, and also suffered shipwreck. *Batuta* however finally reached China by Tibet.

into German by *Kosegarten*, into English by *Professor Lee*, and into French in the Nouveau Journal Asiatique.

These are the only sources respecting India which have been delivered to us by the middle ages.*

A new era commenced when *Vasco di Gama* had discovered the passage by the Cape of Good Hope, and founded *Goa* in the sixteenth century. The Portuguese now penetrated into the southern parts of India, which hitherto had been but little known, and our stores of knowledge were increased.

It is however to the *Missionaries*, and especially to the *Jesuits*, sent by the *Congregatio de propaganda Fide*, that we are really indebted for the best accounts of India in the sixteenth and seventeenth centuries. The most distinguished of those were, *Pere du Halde*, *Bouchet*, *Duisse*, *Tachard*, *Manduit*, *Martin*, *d'Entrecolles*, and *Stephen le Gac*. Their narratives are for the most part collected in the very remarkable work entitled, "Lettres édifiantes par les Missionaires de la Compagnie de Jesus."

* The remarkable journey of *Marco Polo*, at the close of the thirteenth century, was in fact to *China* and *Tibet*, but not to *India*.

After the Jesuits of the Propaganda, two Frenchmen, *Bernier* and *Tavernier*, have given the most correct accounts of India. The former travelled there from 1640 to 1645, under the reign of *Shah Jehan* and that of the celebrated *Aurung Zeb*. His statements are in all respects to be depended upon, and especially in everything relating to *Cashmeer*, where he remained a considerable time.

Tavernier travelled somewhat later, but as he was unacquainted with the oriental languages, his statements are the less to be relied upon.

Anquetil du Perron visited India in the eighteenth century. His chief merit consists in his having brought from India the sacred books of the *Zend-tribes*, and translating them into the French language.

Gentil's "Voyage dans les Mers des Indes" (1660), and *Bailly's* "Traité sur l'Astronomie Indienne" (1785), possess great scientific merit.

It was, however, reserved for the English to communicate the best accounts; and who could be better qualified for this purpose than the people who governed India? *Sir William Jones*, the first President of the Asiatic Society in Calcutta (in the year 1787), prepared the way for this knowledge in a literary point of view. With multifarious European and Oriental learning, Sir William combined the advantage of a thirty years' residence in India, on which account his works are of great value. To cite all the writers after him, who have distinguished themselves in this department, would require an entire catalogue; I therefore confine myself to enumerate merely the names of those authors whose works have been chiefly made use of in the course of this essay. They are the following:—*Sir W. Jones,** *Colebrooke,*† *Crawford,*‡ *Houghton,*§ *Todd,*‖ *Sir John Malcolm,*¶ *Mountstuart Elphinstone,*** *Coleman,*†† *Polier,*‡‡ *Kennedy,*§§ and *Wilson.*‖‖ The other numerous sources which have been employed will be mentioned in their proper places.

* Ordinances of Menu; Asiatic Researches, &c.

† Essay on the Philosophy of the Hindus; Digest of the Hindu Law; Asiatic Researches.

‡ Sketches of Hindostan.

§ Religious Establishment of *Mevar*.

‖ Annals of Rajast'han.

¶ History of Central India and Malva.

** Embassy to Cabul; History of India.

†† Mythology of the Hindoos.

‡‡ Mythologie des Indous.

§§ Researches into Hindoo Mythology.

‖‖ Essay on the Puranas; Asiatic Researches, &c.

GENERAL VIEW OF THE RELIGION OF THE HINDOOS.

THE religion of the Hindoos, which is called the *Brahmin,* is the most *ancient* of the present systems of religion upon the earth, and probably one of the oldest ever known ; in this respect, therefore, it is deserving of a high degree of attention. The doctrine is based upon the books of religion held sacred by the Hindoos, called *Vedas,* written in the ancient *Sanscrit,* which bears the same relation to the present dialects of the Sanscrit, the Hindostanee, Bengalee, Tamul, &c., as the *Gothic* does to the *Swedish,* and the *Latin* to the *French* and *Italian.* The Hindoos maintain that the *Vedas* (four books) are contemporary with the creation, and were revealed by *Brahma* himself. The sacred volume begins with these words:—“ There is only one God, *Brahma,* omnipotent, eternal, omnipresent, the great soul, of which all other gods are but parts.” Nevertheless the *Vedas* do not address their hymns to this only

God, but to things created by him, as the sun, the moon, the stars, the earth, fire, &c.; so that this religion, although *Monotheistic* in its fundamental principle, is tinctured with a kind of *Sabæism*, which probably constituted the early religion at the time when the ancestors of the Hindoos still dwelt in that *country* from which they came to India (from 2500 to 3000 years before Christ). The *Vedas* also contain a *Cosmogony*, the most ancient that is known.

The *second* stadium in the development of the religion of the *Brahmins* commenced about the time when an abstract from the *Vedas*, denominated the *Vedanta*, gave a more decided *form* to the doctrine, and brought it into a closer connexion. This stadium may be termed the *pure Monotheistic* of the religious doctrine of the Hindoos (2000 years before Christ).

The *third* stadium is that when a new Codex, under the name of the laws,* institutions, or ordinances of *Menu*, imparted to the doctrine another character, and brought it from *Monotheism* to the

* *Institutions* is the term employed by most Hindooists, though *Colebrooke*, in his translation of *Menu*, has used the word *ordinances*.

principle of *Pantheism* (See Sir William Jones's Translation of the Laws of Menu, Cap. I. 5, 6, 7, 8); adopted inferior deities (Cap. I. 35), saints (*Menus*) (Cap. I. 36), and genii (Cap. I. 37), and introduced the doctrine of the transmigration of souls (Cap. I. 50, 55). This took place 900 years before Christ.*

The *fourth* stadium, in the development of the Hindoo religion, is that when the *Puranas*† (18 in number) brought the doctrine from the principle of the *Unity* to that of the *Trinity*, or more correctly speaking, combined the principle of the *Trinity* with that of the *Unity*, and moreover adopted the *doctrine of the incarnation.*

The *fifth* stadium is that when the *Upa-Puranas* (the lesser Puranas,‡ which may be compared with the *Legends* of the Roman Catholics) exalted a number of pious men to be *saints* or *demi-gods*, and when the *Poets*, like Homer, in connexion with the *Upa-Puranas*, wove the mythological net which now surrounds the Brahmin doctrine (800 years before Christ).

The *sixth* stadium (which may be denominated

* *Mountstuart Elphinstone*, History of India, Vol. i. pp. 429, 430.

† *Sir William Jones*, Laws of Menu, son of Brahma.

‡ *Wilson*, Essay on the Puranas.

that of the *Reformation*) commenced when the doctrine of the *Buddah's* caused the great schism which at length divided the Brahmin mother-church into two principal branches, of which the creed of the one, namely *Brahmaism*, is acknowledged by far the greater part of the Hindoo nation, and that of the other, namely *Buddhism*, has spread itself, under different denominations, throughout the whole of eastern Asia, as well as into several other parts of the earth (600 years before Christ.)

These different stadia, in the development of the religion of the Hindoos, will, in the course of the present essay, be brought more closely to view. But in the first place I consider it necessary to delineate the *character* of the people, whose religious doctrines I shall afterwards endeavour to lay down.

OF THE DIVISION OF CASTES AMONG THE HINDOOS.

THE foundation stone of the social state of the Hindoos is the *division of Castes.* Its first origin is found in the precepts of Menu, which Brahminical system sets up this division as a religious doctrine. This explains the wonderful phenomena, that a social state, so much opposed to that desire of *equality* so deeply implanted in the human heart, should have been maintained with little change for nearly three thousand years.

According to the sacred writings of the Hindoos, Brahma created *four* kinds of men, each of which forms a peculiar caste. He created the first out of his *head;* this is that of the *Brahmins,* whose business it is to guide and instruct mankind; the second he created out of his *arm, Khetry*

(Ketre), for the purpose of defending and protecting the human race; the third *Vaisyas,* he created out of his *body,* who was to nourish mankind; and the fourth *Sudras,* he created out of his *feet,* in order to serve and obey the other castes.

In conformity with this law it is reserved for the Brahmin alone to *explain* the sacred writings, and he alone can be invested with the *priesthood,* from which the other castes are excluded. He is, moreover, the *physician* (for sickness is a punishment for certain transgressions); he is also the *judge,* for who can be better acquainted with the laws of the land contained in the sacred book.* He alone therefore has the right to explain them.

Together with these occupations, which belong to him *exclusively,* the Brahmin can also exercise those which appertain to the next two castes; he can bear *arms* like the *Khetrys,* and follow trade like the *Vaisyas.*

From these various employments of the Brahmins arise the different classes which are found among them. The highest class is that which

* The sacred books of the Hindoos, especially the Institutions of *Menu,* contain, like the *Alcoran,* both criminal and civil laws, as well as the precepts of religion.

expounds the sacred writings (the Priests). Its members are treated with the greatest reverence even by kings; their lands are exempt from all taxes, and they themselves from corporal punishment; to kill one of these Brahmins is the greatest of crimes. With these *privileges* the Brahmins however are subjected to such severe *duties*, that (celibacy excepted) very few of the Catholic monks can bear a comparison with them. The Brahmin must spend a number of years in the house of his instructor (*Guru*), until he can well expound the *Vedas*, which is a long and tedious study. Then only he may, or rather he *must*, marry, and become the father of a family. His daily life is bound by a strict ritual; the many prayers, ablutions, and sacrifices imposed upon the Brahmin demand a great portion of his time, as the facility with which he may defile himself (which must be atoned for by penance) requires uncommon vigilance. They may not eat with one of a lower caste, no not even with a prince; they are not allowed to kill any living animal unless for sacrifice; they may not eat any meat but what is sacrificed. In old age it is a rule, or at least a custom, for the Brahmins to go into solitude, and to devote themselves to *self-beholding* (contemplation), whereby alone *Nirvani* (*absorption* into the Supreme Being) can be obtained. They have an *hierarchical discipline*, which exposes them to severe punishments; but this is necessary, as the number of Brahmins engaged in the service of the temples is very considerable, and in *Jagernaut* amounts to more than 3000.

It is remarkable how the Brahmin is distinguished, throughout the whole of India, from the lower castes, by a *lighter* and finer colour, by more noble features, and by a larger and more beautiful figure.

Next to the Brahmin-caste comes that of the *Khetry* or *Warriors*. This caste has undergone great changes, owing to the numerous conquests to which India has been exposed. Under such circumstances this caste could not continue in its *old form*, for it was necessarily first affected by the storm; it has in consequence almost ceased to be a caste, and transformed itself rather into a tribe, exercising together with the profession of war the more peaceful occupations of trade, husbandry, and business. All the inhabitants of *Rayasthan*, (*Raypoot*), belong to the Khetry-caste, as also those of *Malva, Bundelkund, Oude, Punjab,* and *Merva.* They resemble in this respect the *Biscayans* in Spain, who *to a man* insist that they are nobles. The law allows the Khetry to *hear the Vedas,* but not to *read* them, and still less to *expound* them. They must *give* alms, but not receive them; they must flee sensual pleasures, and live *frugally* as becomes a warrior. With few exceptions, the *Kings* and *Princes* of India belong to this caste, which in this respect may be considered as the first, although, according to the laws of *Menu,* it is subordinate to the caste of the Brahmins.

The *Vaisyas* form the *industrious* caste, which comprises *merchants, tradesmen,* and *husbandmen.* Of these occupations, however, each constitutes a particular *branch* of the common caste, and they fall among themselves into a multitude of *subdivisions,* which, in the class of tradesmen (consisting of goldsmiths, joiners, carpenters, potters, &c.), correspond pretty nearly to our *companies* or *guilds,* and also in many respects follow the same regulations. In Bengal, where the division of castes is more strictly observed than in the other parts of India, these subdivisions do not intermingle with each other, not even by *marriage;* so that goldsmiths, joiners, potters, and others, all form their peculiar caste.

The *Brahmins*, *Khetrys*, and *Vaisyas*, wear a *girdle* or *cord*, called *zenaar*, which is different for each particular caste. They are termed, in the laws of *Menu*, the twice-born, or the new-born, because the girding with the cord is regarded as a new birth.

The fourth caste, the *Sudras*, belongs to the but once-born, for they are not girded with the cord. A *Sudra*, says *Menu*, acts best if he serves a Brahmin, and next a Khetry; and lastly, a Vaisya. If he finds no opportunity of serving any of these, let him follow a useful trade. He who faithfully *serves a Brahmin, shall, in a future metempsychosis, come into a higher caste.*

The laws of Menu allow *mixed marriages* to the three higher castes, yet only at the *second marriage*, when a man of a *higher* caste can take a wife from a *lower;* but a lady of a *higher* caste can never marry with a man of a lower. To belong to the same caste as the father, the son must have a mother of the like caste; the son of a Brahmin must therefore, in order to belong to the Brahmin caste, also have a Brahmin mother. The *Sudras* can only marry within their own caste; a mixture of Sudras with a higher caste produces *Mandras,* who are considered as an *unclean* caste. The most impure of all are the *Pahrias,* for they are *without* caste. The degradation of a *Pahria* extends so far, that even his *shadow,* if it falls upon a Brahmin, *defiles* the latter, and obliges him to plunge into the sacred waters of the Ganges, the Sarju, or the Nerbudda, in order to wash off the defilement.

It is owing to mixed marriages that the number of castes has gradually increased to such an extent, that in Bengal they now amount to 84, each with a particular *name* and *occupation.*

The greatest calamity that can befall a Hindoo, is to *lose caste,* to which he can be sentenced by a court of justice. In this case the sight of him is avoided; he is driven away wherever he shows himself. In comparison of this, *the bann of the middle ages was a trifle.*

The *castes* of India cannot be compared with the *Classes* in Europe. The caste of the Brahmins (the spiritual order) is *hereditary,* which is not the case with the Christian Priesthood, which springs from the *mass of the people,* and opens its ranks to the poor as well as the rich,—to the plebeian as well as the patrician. Still less can the caste of the Brahmins be compared with the nobility of Europe; the latter is essentially *knightly* and *martial.* The caste of the Brahmins is, on the contrary, a *didactic order*, of a peaceful nature, forbidden even to shed blood, and subjected to the *severest trials* in its youth, to the most abstemious conduct in its manhood, and to the life of an anchorite in its old age. The privileges of the Brahmins therefore extend only to the *intellectual* world, and not to the *material,*—to *power*, *honour*, or *wealth.*

Neither can the caste of the *Khetrys* or *warriors* be compared with the *nobility* of Europe, since its privileges over the other castes frequently consist only in being allowed, as *common soldiers,* to shed their blood in the service of their masters. The *Khetry* therefore possesses none of those privileges which the *nobility* enjoy in most of the European states.

Since, then, neither the caste of the *Khetrys*, nor that of the Brahmins, still less any other, can be compared with the nobility of Europe, or correspond to the idea of an *aristocracy*, it follows that this element is entirely wanting in the social state of the Hindoos; and this serves to explain the reason why the *Despotism* of the Indian *Princes* has been so *unbounded*, and why the *people*, incapable of making any resistance (for which purpose *points of union* and *support* are requisite), have done so little to defend their country and their hearths against *foreign* invaders, who, during many centuries, have subjugated it, and of whom the Affghans, the Moguls, and the Persians, in the fullest sense have verified the words of *Brennus*—*Væ victis!*

Every page of the history of the world shows that those states which are destitute of the aristocratic element (understood in its nobler sense, namely, as *open to every kind of merit*, and not *exclusive*, like the Roman or Venetian Patriciate), have soon degenerated either to the *despotism of an individual*, or to the still more dangerous *despotism of polyarchy*.

History likewise shows, that all those nations which have performed *great actions*, and still *preserved their liberty*, from the Roman down to the British, have possessed within themselves a more or less *influential aristocracy;* for the element which advances in the most persevering and steady manner, is without doubt the *aristocratic.* The mass of the people may be misled by their ignorance, or be carried away by the impressions of the moment; kings may be seduced by those around them, and by their passions; may be *inconstant* in their purposes,—they are *mortal;* an *aristocratic corporation* is *too numerous* to be misled like a king;—*not numerous enough* to be carried away by passion, like the mass of the people; it resembles a man *firm and enlightened, who never dies.**

* The necessity of an aristocratic element in a lawful but free state, as a counterpoise to the democratic, has been doubted by no statesman or philosopher, from *Cicero* (de Republica) down to *Tocqueville* (Démocratie en Amérique).

OF THE HIGH ANTIQUITY OF THE BRAHMINICAL RELIGION, AND OF THE EARLY DEVELOPMENT OF CULTURE AND OF SCIENCE IN INDIA.

THE most ancient book of religion of the *Hindoos* is called *Veda** (four books), and, according to the assertion of the Hindoos, is a revelation from Brahma himself. *Viasa*† has made an abstract of it, called *Vedanta*, which now forms the basis of the Brahmin doctrine.

The right *age* of the *Vedas* has long formed an unsolved problem for the learned of Europe, some of whom have considered it to belong to a very early period; others again as being more recent. At length a *fixed point* has been found from which to proceed in the *Hindoo chronology*; this

* In the plural *Vedas*. In the British Museum, there is a complete copy of the Vedas, which was brought from *Jeyopoor* in India by Colonel Polier; it is in fourteen folio volumes. There is another complete copy in the Royal Library at Paris, written on palm-leaves.

† *Viasa* is considered by some not as a proper name but as an appellative, signifying the *Commentator*.

is the reign of king *Nandi,* which commenced 400 years before Christ.*

The sixth king before *Nandi* was *Ajata Satru.* If we reckon a reign of 30 years for each of these six kings, *Nandi's* included, there results a period of 210 years, which, added to the 400 years before Christ when *Nandi* began to reign, give for the commencement of the reign of *Ajata Satru* the date of 610 years before Christ.

Four different *Puranas* specify in accordance the succession of forty-seven kings,† who reigned before *Ajata Satru,* from the great war between the royal races of the *Panduides* and the *Kurnides,* which is celebrated in the famous poem *Mâhabhârata,* where *Krischna* appears as the hero of the former.

If here also we take an average of thirty years'

* A *date* corresponding to this point of time has recently been discovered in an inscription on *Tiruz Shah's* column in Delhi; a second on a rock at *Girnas,* by the Rev.—Stevenson; and a third in *Däuli,* by Capt. Kittoe. Several inscriptions on *medals* (for the explanation of which we are indebted to the distinguished orientalist Professor *Lassen* of Bonn) bear testimony to this date of *Nandi's* reign.

† See *Mountstuart Elphinstone's* History of India, 1841, vol. i. page 267. The *Puranas* also mention the number of years each king reigned, and these united make 1500 years, which gives an average of thirty-one years for each king. We have taken an average of thirty years.

reign for each king, (which agrees with the usual proportion in India), there results a period of 1410 years, which, added to the time when *Ajata Satru* began to reign (610 years before Christ), shows that the great war took place about 2000 years before Christ. It was at this time *Viasa* made his abridgment of the *Vedas* under the name of the *Vedanta,* a circumstance he himself mentions in his work.

Hence we find that the *Vedanta* was composed 2000 years before Christ. With this guidance we can now find the correct age of the *Vedas,* of which the *Vedanta,* by *Viasa,* as has been already stated, is but an abstract.

The Hindoos assert that the *Vedas* are several *thousand years* older than the *Vedanta.* This seems an exaggeration. However, the *Vedas* must be much older than the *Vedanta,* since the author of the latter gives, as a reason for undertaking his work, that *the language of the Vedas was obsolete and unintelligible to the people of his age.*

This *circumstance* presupposes (especially among a people like the Hindoos, with the spirit of *stability* which prevailed among them) a period of at least some centuries. Let us take 500, which, added to the 2000 years before Christ, when the *Vedanta* was written, gives an age of 2500 years before Christ for the *Vedas.** We must, moreover, not overlook the circumstance, that the first book of the *Vedas* is written in a far more ancient *Sanscrit* than the three other books; let us take three centuries for this difference of language, and we find that the first book of the *Vedas* (which, like the first book of Moses, or *Genesis*, contains the *cosmogony* of the Hindoo system of religion) must *be* 2800 *years older than the birth of Christ,*† which, according to the Hebrew computation, is 800 years before the time of *Abraham.* In so remote an age the Hindoos already possessed *written books of religion.*

The abstract metaphysical questions which are treated of in these books, prove what a high degree of culture this people had at that time already attained. The *Vedas* thus express themselves:

The angels assembled themselves before the throne of the Almighty, and said with sub-

* *Sir William Jones* computes the age of the *Vedas* to be about the same, but from different grounds.

† Why we are so particular with regard to this chronological computation, will be seen in the sequel.

mission: "O *Ruder*,* we wish to know how the soul is united with the body; how the world was created; how the soul comes into conjunction with the Divine; what is the magnitude and measure of the universe, of the sun, the moon, the stars, and the earth; and what is the end of all?" The answers given by *Ruder* worthily correspond to the depth of the questions proposed. Remarkable is the precision with which the *immortality of the soul*, and its *existence when separate from the body*, is expressed in the sacred writings of the Hindoos, and not merely as a *philosophical* proposition, but as a *doctrine of religion*.

In this respect the Hindoos were far in advance of the philosophers of Greece and Rome, who considered the immortality of the soul as *problematical*. Of this we find proofs in the review of their opinions, as given by *Cicero* in his excellent treatise *de Senectute*, and also in his *Quæstiones Tusculanæ*. He there shows the uncertainty which prevailed among the ancient philosophers on this important point. They perceived, indeed, that as man's *material* qualities have no connexion with *thought, memory, imagi-*

* That is one of the names of God.

nation, &c., that these qualities must therefore appertain to something separate from the body, of a *spiritual, indissoluble*, and *immortal nature*, which, after its release from its bodily prison, elevates itself above time and space to those higher spheres where it can attain a degree of happiness, wisdom, and perfection, of which the *material* part of man is insusceptible. Hence these philosophers drew the *rash* conclusion, that the soul, independent of its future *immortality*, had also *existed from eternity* (had pre-existed), and consequently must be an *emanation* from the *infinite, eternal Spirit*, who fills the universe, having proceeded from the latter as beams from the sun, without diminishing its light, power, and warmth. This view of the soul's immortality leads, however, to the idea, that the object must rather be the quantity of bliss, wisdom, and perfection which the soul of mankind can *collectively* attain, than its *identity*, with regard to the *individual*, which may come to the enjoyment of it.

According to this view, *Socrates* at the hour of his death, and *Socrates* thousands of years afterwards, when infinitely advanced in perfection, could not be the same person, at least not otherwise than what *Newton* was as a child, compared with *Newton* when he discovered the motive powers of the planetary system; and in such case how could Socrates in *Elysium* concern himself about Socrates in Athens!

But this annihilates what is most dear to man, the hope of his *individual* continuance after death,—a hope which, being grounded upon the rock of revelation, is of more value to him than all that metaphysical speculation can offer in its place.

The Hindoos thus acknowledged the *immortality of the soul* as an *article of religion* long before the time when a small number of *philosophers* in Greece and Rome had elevated themselves to this view, and when the mass of the people, sunk in materialism, sought at the altars of their gods nothing but *temporal happiness*.

In a *metaphysical* point of view we find among the Hindoos all the *fundamental ideas* of those vast systems which, regarded merely as the offspring of fantasy, nevertheless inspire admiration on account of the boldness of their flight, and of the faculty of the human mind to elevate itself to such remote etherial regions. We find among them all the principal doctrines of *Pantheism*,

Spinozism, and *Hegelianism*; of *God* as being one with the *universe*;* of the eternal Spirit descended on earth in the *whole spiritual life* of mankind; of the return of the emanative sparks after death to their divine origin; of the uninterrupted alternation between *life* and *death*, which is nothing else but a transition between different modes of existence. All this we find again among the philosophers of the Hindoos, exhibited as clearly as by our modern philosophers, *more than three thousand years since.*

The *early* civilization of India is also evident from the above-mentioned ancient code of laws, called *The Institutions of Menu*, which, in addition to religious precepts, also contains, like the Koran, civil laws. It prescribes orders respecting commerce, trade, and industry, which are *still* convenient; it fixes a rate of interest for money lent, prescribes a law respecting bills of exchange, and makes mention of a representative

* To conceive God without any other individuality than that of the *universe*, is to resolve the Deity into a negation. To represent God as the *soul* of the *universe*, encompassed by the universe, as the soul of man is encompassed by his body, is different. In this case the universe is the *manifestation* of God, and not his own essence.

paper coin, and all this a thousand years before our era.

The Hindoos assert that *Bhrim* created the earth in the course of four great periods, called *Yugs;* the first of which, *Satya Yug*, lasted 1,728,000 years; the second, *Trita Yug*, 1,296,000; the third, *Dvapa Yug*, 864,000; and the fourth, *Kali Yug* (the present period), will continue 432,000 years.*

A great diversity prevails in determining the *commencement* of the last *Yug*. According to *Gentil, W. Jones,* and *Niebuhr*, it commenced 3100 years before Christ; but according to *Bentley* not earlier than 1003 years before Christ. The first *Yug* contains the Myth of the deluge; the second the history of the commencement of the Indian empires, by the dynasties of the children of the sun and of the moon. *Brigha, Indra, Pura, Wiswamitra,* and *Parasa Rama* were living in this *Yug; Vyasa* in the third *Yug*.

* The computation here adopted is considered by the best oriental authorities (Colebrooke, Niebuhr, Elphinstone, &c.) as agreeing most closely with the sacred books of the Hindoos. There are, however, other versions of these eras, specially Buddhistical, which deviate considerably from the former; yet the greater or less fundamental number, 432, is found in them all, multiplied a number of times.

The *Vedas* do not mention the *Yugs* at all. The Brahmins consider the numbers of the first three *Yugs* as an astronomical calculation.

They all proceed from the number 432, which is the arithmetical centre of the Indian system, and indicates the revolutions of the heavens. Now, as the Brahmins assume that the equinox always takes place 55 seconds earlier every year, a period of 24,000 years is required for every such total revolution of the heavens; and as each number of the four epochs of the world may be divided by 24,000, it is clear that these periods express the motion of the stars.

The antiquity of the Hindoo *Astronomy* has long been a disputed point among the learned of Europe. *Cassini*,* *Bailly*,† *Gentil*,‡ and *Playfair*§ maintain, that there are Hindoo observations extant which must have been made more than 3000 years before Christ, and which evince even then *a very high degree* of astronomical science.‖ Other learned men, among whom are *La Place*,¶

* Traité sur l'Astronomie.

† Histoire de l'Astronomie Ancienne; and Astronomie des Indiennes.

‡ Voyage dans les Mers des Indes.

§ Astronomy of the Hindoos.

‖ Oriental Magazine, vol. v. p. 245.

¶ Exposé du Systême du Monde.

Bentley,* and *Delambre*,† deny the *authenticity* of these observations, and consequently do not admit the conclusions thence deduced.

But these learned men, and Bentley especially, acknowledge the great antiquity of the Hindoo observations, although they do not consider them so ancient as is asserted by Bailly and Playfair. Bentley says, in his posthumous treatise, entitled, " History of Astronomy," *that the division of the Ecliptic by the Hindoos into twenty-seven mansions, must have been made* 1442 *years before Christ*, which shows that they had even at that time attained a high degree of astronomical science. This was two centuries earlier than the Argonautic expedition, the first occasion on which the Greeks make mention of astronomical observations made by themselves.

Davis, who has also taken up this question, calculates that the celebrated Hindoo astronomer *Parasura*, judging from the *observations* made by him, must have lived 1391 years before Christ (Asiatic Researches, vol. ii. p. 288), and consequently had read in the divine book of the hea-

* Antiquity of the Surrya Siddhanta; and Astronomy of the Hindoos.

† Astronomie des Peuples de l'Asie.

venly firmament, long before the Chaldees, the Arabs, and the Greeks.

Thus, if we reduce the age of the Hindoo observations as computed by Bailly from 3000 years before Christ to the time calculated by Bentley, La Place, and Delambre, namely, 1442 years before our chronology, we have at all events this fact, that the Hindoos *preceded* all other nations in the application of the higher astronomy.

According to the astronomical calculations of the Hindoos, the present period of the world, *Kali-Yug*,* commenced 3102 years before the birth of Christ, on the 20th of February, at 2 hours, 27 minutes, and 30 seconds, the time being thus calculated to minutes and seconds. They say that a *conjunction of the planets* then took place, and their tables show this conjunction. Bailly states, that Jupiter and Mercury were then in the same degree of the ecliptic, Mars at a distance of only eight, and Saturn of seven degrees; whence it follows, that at the point of time given by the Brahmins as the commencement of *Kali-Yug*, the four planets above mentioned must have been

* *Kali-Yug* signifies the age of trouble, the iron age of the ancient Greeks.

successively concealed by the rays of the sun (first Saturn, then Mars, afterwards Jupiter, and lastly Mercury). They thus showed themselves in *conjunction;* and although Venus could not then be seen, it was natural to say, *that a conjunction of the planets then took place.* The calculation of the Brahmins is so exactly confirmed by our own astronomical tables, says Bailly, that nothing but an *actual observation* could have given so correspondent a result. He further informs us, that Laubère, who was sent by Louis XIV. as ambassador to the King of Siam, brought home, in the year 1687, astronomical tables of solar eclipses, and that other similar tables were sent to Europe by Patouillet (a missionary in the Carnatic), and by Gentil, which latter were obtained from the Brahmins in Tirvalore,* and that they *all perfectly agree in their calculations, although received from different persons, at different times, and from places in India remote from each other.*

On these tables Bailly makes the following observation:—

* What Cuvier cites in this respect (Discours sur les Révolutions du Globe, p. 235) is according to Bentley, but corrected by Bentley himself in his last work, referred to above. (See the Oriental Magazine, vol. v. p. 245, &c.)

"The *motion* calculated by the Brahmins during the long space of 4383 years (the period elapsed between these calculations and Bailly's) varies not a *single minute* from the tables of Cassini and Meyer; and as the tables brought to Europe by Laubère in 1687, under Louis XIV., are older than those of Cassini and Meyer, the accordance between them must be the result of *mutual* and exact astronomical observations."

Another proof may also be alleged in this respect, namely, that the Indian tables give the same annual variation of the moon as that discovered by Tycho Brahe; a variation unknown to the school of Alexandria, and also to the Arabs, who followed the calculations of this school.

These facts sufficiently show the great antiquity and distinguished station of astronomical science among the Hindoos of past ages.

Geometry had also made similar early progress with this nation.

We find in *Ayen Akbaree*, a journal of the Emperor Akbar,* that the Hindoos of former

* He was born in 1555, and died in 1605, and was the father of Shah Jehan, and grandfather of the celebrated Aurung-Zeb.

times assumed the diameter of a circle to be to its periphery as 1250 to 3927. The ratio of 1250 to 3927 is a very close approximation to the quadrature of the circle, and differs very little from that given by Metius, of 113 to 355. In order to obtain the result thus found by the Brahmins, even in the most elementary and simplest way, it is necessary to inscribe in a circle a polygon of 768 sides, an operation which cannot be performed arithmetically without the knowledge of some peculiar properties of this curved line, and at least an extraction of the square root of the ninth power, each to ten places of decimals. The Greeks and Arabs have not given anything so approximate.

But if it be true that thc Hindoos, more than 3000 years before Christ, according to Bailly's calculation (or even if the latter be reduced to 1442 years before Christ, according to the calculation of Bentley), had attained so high a degree of *astronomical* and *geometrical* learning, how many centuries *earlier* must the commencement of their culture have been, since the human mind advances only step by step on the path of science!

Besides the proofs adduced of the great antiquity of the civilization of the Hindoos, there are others perhaps still stronger; namely, those gigantic temples hewn out of lofty rocks, with the most incredible labour, at *Elephanta*, at *Ellora*, and several other places; which, with regard to the vastness of the undertaking, may be compared with the pyramids, and in an architectural respect even surpass them.

Let us now examine if this high degree of culture, at so remote a period, was of Hindoo origin, and genuine in India, or borrowed from any other nation, preceding the *Hindoos* in art, science, and civilization. Only two nations can in this respect vie with the Hindoos, namely, the Egyptians and the Chinese.

The Persians (the Zend-people) may possibly emulate them with respect to the antiquity of their *religion*, but there is no trace among them of a degree of science, art, and civilization, at all comparable with the antiquity of that of the Hindoos.

The Phenicians derived their religion and their culture from Egypt; the Chaldeans, the Babylonians, and the inhabitants of Cholchis, theirs from India. The progress of the Hebrews and the Greeks was later than that of Hindostan. Egypt and China are consequently the only countries, which, in this respect, can vie with the Hindoos.

As all the ancient legislators rested their systems upon religious sanction, and strove to found the institutions of *time* upon the basis of *eternity*, the surest way to ascertain which nation preceded the rest in civilization, is to examine the relative antiquity of its religion.

On a comparison of the religion of the Egyptians and Hindoos, we are struck by the resemblances between them. Both proceed from *monotheistic* principles, and degenerate into a *polytheistic* heathenism, though rather of a *symbolic* than of a *positive* character. They both adopt the principle of the *Trinity*, combined with that of the *Unity*.* Both assume the pre-ex-

* According to the discoveries of Champollion in the temple of *Kalabski* in Nubia (in 1829), it was a whole series of *Triads of Gods* that the Egyptians worshipped; the first link of these Triads was *Amon-ras* (the Genitor), *Muth* (the Genitrix), and *Chous* (the Son or the Production), a super-terrestrial *Triad*, which was converted into the more earthly one of *Osiris*, *Isis*, and *Horus*, with the same symbols as the preceding; this Triad afterwards multiplied itself down to a concluding Triad, perfectly corresponding to the primitive.

istence of the soul, its emanation from the Divine essence, its transmigration (metempsychosis), and its return after death to its Divine origin.* They both adopt the *division of castes*, and nearly upon the same grounds—of Priests (Brahmins), Warriors, Traders, and Agriculturists, and regarded this division as a religious principle.†

Even the symbols are the same on the shores of the *Ganges* and the *Nile*. Thus we find the *Lingam* of the *Siva-temples* of India, in the *Phallus* of the *Ammon-temples* of Egypt; a symbol also met with on the head-dress of the Egyptian gods.‡ We find the *lotus-flower*,§ as the symbol of the sun, both in India and in Egypt; and we find symbols of the immortality of the soul in both countries. The power of rendering barren women fruitful, ascribed to the temples of *Siva* in India, was also ascribed to the temples of *Ammon* in Egypt; a belief retained to our

* Vide the Timæus of Plato and Herodotus.

† Vide Herodotus, Strabo, and Aristotle.

‡ See Champollion Figeac's work on Egypt, plate 33, fig. 7, *Osiris*, and plate 91, *Horus*, the head-dresses of which represent the Hindoo *Lingam*.

§ *Nymphæa*, which closes at the setting and opens at the rising of the sun.

days, for the Bedouin women may be still seen wandering around the temple of Ammon, for the purpose of obtaining this blessing.

Even several *names* of Hindoo mythology are recognized in Egypt; thus *Ammon*, the supreme god of the Egyptians, corresponds to the *Aum* of the Hindoos; and the Brahminical *Siva* is found in the temple to which *Alexander the Great* made his pilgrimage from Egypt, and which yet bears this name.*

These accordances between the religion of the Brahmins and that of the ancient Egyptians, leave no doubt that *the one takes its origin from the other; but which of the two is the root, may still be questionable.* We will therefore proceed to examine this point. The chronological dates seem to be in favour of Egypt. According to *Manetho's* tables of kings, which were found in the temple where he officiated,† the great

* According to the accounts of the priests in *Sais* to Herodotus, two priestesses or prophetesses were sent from the great temple of Ammon in Thebes, to select spots in which sacerdotal temples might be erected; the one pointed out *Siva* in the Lybian desert, the other *Dodona* (Bodona) in *Epirus*. The Greeks transformed these prophetesses into *pigeons*, the one white and the other black.

† *Manetho* was the high-priest in Heliopolis 360 years before

pyramid of *Gizeh* was built by *Soufi,* the first Pharaoh of the fourth dynasty, who reigned 5000 years before Christ (see the subjoined table), a statement confirmed by the drawings discovered in the interior of the same pyramid by Colonel *Wyse* (in 1838), showing the *position of the stars* when the pyramid was erected, which position, according to the calculation made by *Thilorier* (in 1840), must have taken place 4950 years before Christ, consequently at the time given by Manetho for the reign of *Soufi.*

The pyramid of *Gizeh* presents, however, no sculptures or drawings which lead to the supposition that the *religion* of the Egyptians, at that time, was the same as that which a thousand years later was celebrated in the *temples* of Egypt, and which exhibits so much resemblance to the religion of the Hindoos. The immense age of the pyramids of *Gizeh* is consequently no proof that the *religion* of the Egyptians was older than that of the Hindoos.

Christ. His annals have been lost, but portions of them are preserved in the extracts given of them by *Josephus*, *Julius Africanus*, and *Eusebius*.

On the other hand, the derivation of the religion of the Egyptians from that of the Hindoos may be proved by the following grounds:—

1st. It is testified by Herodotus, Plato, Solon, Pythagoras, and Philostratus, that the religion of Egypt proceeded from *India.*

2ndly. It is testified by Niebuhr, Valentia, Champollion, and Waddington, that the temples of Upper Egypt are of greater antiquity than those of Lower Egypt; that the temples in Meroe are more ancient than those of Elephantine and Thebes; these more ancient than the temples of Tentyra and Abydos; and these again more ancient than those of Memphis, Heliopolis, and Sais;* that, consequently, the religion of Egypt, according to the testimony of these monuments, proceeded *from the south,* which cannot be from any other land than from *Ethiopia* and *Meroe,* to which country it came from *India,* as testified by the above-named Greek authorities.†

* See Niebuhr's Travels, Lord Valentia's Travels in India, and Waddington's Visit to Ethiopia (1822).

† There are temples in *Lybia, Ethiopia,* and *Upper Egypt,* of far more recent date; but these were constructed by *Greek* colonists, under the *Ptolemies,* and ought not to be confounded with the real Egyptian temples; their architecture is also Grecian.

3rdly. The chronicles, found in the temples of Abydos and Sais, and which have been transmitted to us by Josephus, Julius Africanus, and Eusebius, all testify that the religious system of the Egyptians proceeded from India.*

4thly. The continent of Asia, with its vast mountain and table lands, possesses greater claims to be regarded as the locality where mankind first spread, than the narrow valley of the Nile, bounded by deserts.

5thly. The earliest traditions of the most ancient nations of the globe point to the high table-lands of Central Asia as the first *home* of the human race, and this high-land is close to India, but far from Egypt; India must, consequently, have been inhabited *earlier*, and must therefore have developed its religion and culture earlier than Egypt.†

* Probably along the south coast of Arabia. The passage thither from the Indus was inconsiderable, and that from Arabia to Ethiopia by the straits of Bab-el-Mandel still less. The ancient geographers called by the name of Ethiopia all that part of Africa which now constitutes Nubia, Abyssinia, Senaar, Darfur, and Dongola.

† Frederic Schlegel expresses himself in the following terms in his work entitled *Sprache und Weisheit der Indier*. The real primordial land is to be sought for in the northern parts of India, in the Bactrian high-land between India, Persia, and the sources of *Gihon* (Oxus), where everything combines to point

6thly. We have *Hindoo* chronologies (besides those of the *Puranas* concerning the *Yugs*, which are nothing but astronomical allegories), which go still further back in time than the tables of the Egyptian kings according to *Manetho*.

Megasthenes, the envoy of Alexander to *K'andragupso* (the Greeks call him Sandrogypsos,) king of the Gangarides, discovered chronological tables at *Polybothra* the residence of this king, which contain a series of no less than 153 kings, with all their names, from *Dionysius* (if there ever was a king of this name in India), to *K'andragupso*, and specifying the duration of the reigns of every one of those kings, together amounting to 6451 years, which would place the reign of Dionysius nearly 7000 years before Christ, and consequently one thousand years before the *eldest* king found on the Egyptian tables of *Manetho* (viz., the head of the *Tinite Thebaine* dynasty), who reigned 5867 years before Christ, and 2000 years before *Soufi*, the founder of the Gizeh Pyramid.

out a common origin of our faith, our knowledge, and our history. This seems also to be the opinion of Baron Alexander Humboldt, and of Chevalier de Bunzen, two first-rate authorities.

7thly. There is a tradition among the Abyssinians, which they say they have possessed from time immemorial, and which is still equally received among the Jews and Christians of that country, that the first inhabitants (they say *Cush*, grandson of Noah, with his family) came over the chain of mountains, which separates the high lands of Abyssinia from the Red Sea and the Strait of Babel Mandel, from a remote southern country. The tradition further says, that they built the city of *Axum*, early in the days of Abraham, and that from thence they spread themselves, following the river Nile downwards, until they became (as Josephus says) the *Meroetes*; viz. the inhabitants of that part of *Nubia*, which, being situated between the *Nile* and its conflux the *Atbara*, forms what is commonly called the island of *Meroe*, from which they spread farther down the river, to *Egypt*.

It appears, from the above-mentioned grounds, that the Hindoos have a greater claim to the primogeniture of religion, and consequently to the primogeniture of civilization, than the people of ancient Egypt.

We now proceed to the history of China.

The history of China, that is to say the certain period thereof, does not reach further back than the reign of *Schihoang* (230 to 250 years before Christ), a very recent period compared with India,* in consequence of this emperor *Schihoang* having ordered all the historical writings then extant to be burnt. One manuscript, however (named *Schuking*), was saved in the sarcophagus of *Koong-fu-tse* † (Confucius). It is this that now forms the only source for the history of China before *Schihoang*.

According to this document, the Chinese nation is descended from the high-land to the north-west of China (Mongolia), whence, at a very remote period, their ancestors had come down into the plains of China, along the valleys formed by the rivers *Hoangho* and *Hoiho*. *Fohi* is mentioned as the leader of the Chinese nation at that period, but the time when he lived is not determined. That it was very remote, appears from the

* The records of China extend indeed to the reign of *Vuvang*, 1100 years before Christ, but they are only founded on *tradition*.

† *Koong-fu-tse* was born 550 years before Christ, consequently 400 years later than *Menu*, the law-giver of India.

fact that the Indian *Menu* has named *Fohi* as an ancient chief of the people of China (Tsina).

It is after this manuscript, that Koong-fu-tse composed the history of China, in which it is stated that *Chinong*, the twelfth successor of *Fohi*, reigned 2000 years before Christ. This statement is, however, uncertain, and leaves the question undecided, which of the two nations, the Chinese or the Hindoos, is the elder in civilization.

What may be said with certainty is, that the *religion* of China came from India, namely, that religion professed by the mass of the nation; for the doctrine of Koong-fu-tse, although the *state* religion, is only professed by the higher classes; ***Buddhism*** is the faith of the people, and came to China by two different routes, and in two different forms; in the one it is called the doctrine of *Fo* (*Fuh-Budh*), in the other that of *Dalai-Lama*.

Fo (Budh), a holy man, came to China sixty years after the birth of Christ,* and began to publish his doctrine, which by degrees spread itself so considerably, that the far greater part of

* Under the reign of *Ming-ty* and the dynasty *Hân*.

the immense population of China, now profess this faith.

Not long after the arrival of Budh, the first conquest of China by the Mongolian Tartars took place; and as these were worshippers of *Dalai-Lama,* a branch of *Buddhism,* this doctrine was introduced into China, and is still there professed by all those of Tartaric origin.

The two above-named *Sects* form now a mass of no less than 300,000,000 of *Buddhists,* whilst the doctrines of Koong-fu-tse, with several kinds of *rationalists,* comprise about 20 millions, the population, according to Gutzlaf, being estimated at 320,000,000.

The Chinese nation gives here a new proof that the *bulk* of a people cannot be satisfied with a religion founded only upon *rational* grounds, but eagerly seeks for a *supernatural* creed, which addresses itself more to the human heart, and teaches more consolatory convictions than those of cold philosophy. This fact is so much the more remarkable, as the doctrine of Confucius is 600 years older in China than that of Fo, and alone entitles to admission to the offices of the state; nevertheless, 300 millions bend the knee to the Trimurti of Buddha, whilst few adhere to the doctrines of philosophy.

What has been briefly stated here may be sufficient to show that no nation on earth can vie with the Hindoos in respect to the *antiquity* of their *religion,* and the *antiquity* of their *civilization.*

But if civilization in India is *very ancient,* it has been so much the more *stationary.* There, also, time hastens forwards on his pinions, but is unable to put in motion the *stiff form;* and the Hindoo stands still at the altars of his gods, as he did 4000 years ago, at the time of the *Panduits* and the *Kurnids,* of *Krischna* and of *Rama.* In Europe everything is changeable, is transient; in India all is stationary, is immoveable, like the temples of Ellora, hewn out of the rocks.

THE RELIGION OF THE HINDOOS.

ACCORDING to what has been already stated, the Vedas form the basis of the religion of the Hindoos. They consist of four distinct parts or books. Each Veda is composed of three divisions, the first of which, called Mantra, contains hymns and prayers to the Almighty; the second, named Brahmana, consists of the precepts of religion and theological arguments; and the third, termed Upanishad, forms an abstract of the two preceding.* The Vedas were not composed by one and the same author, but by several, whose names are frequently given beneath the hymns and precepts of which they are the authors.

To judge from the difference of the language, many centuries must have elapsed between the

* There is a complete copy of the Vedas preserved in the British Museum, in fourteen folio volumes, which together form the four books of which the Vedas consist. There is another copy on palm leaves, with Talinna characters, and a third with Devanagari characters, in the library at Paris. These are probably the only complete sets found in Europe.

composition of the first and last books of the Vedas. The Hindoos maintain that the Vedas are contemporaneous with the creation, and were revealed by Brahma himself.* Written in a metaphorical style, they are not clear, and are often contradictory. Viasa, who is himself regarded as a holy being, made an abridgment of them 2000 years before Christ, called Vedanta, that is to say, an explanation of the Vedas, which now constitutes the proper sacred scripture of the Hindoos, studied by the Brahmins.

Only smaller portions of the Vedas have been translated into the European languages. Colebrooke's English versions are most to be depended upon; and although they are insufficient to enable us to form a right judgment of the actual contents of the doctrine exhibited, it is evident, however, that it was a *monotheism*, encompassed by a *Sabæistic* form, or founded upon it.

The Vedas express themselves in the following manner: "The angels assembled around the throne

* Properly *Brahm* or *Brihm*, as the Creator of the world; he is also denoted by the mysterious monosyllable *Aum*, which, out of reverence, no Hindoo may pronounce aloud. Brahma, on the contrary, is the name of the first person in the Hindoo *Trimurti*, or triad of gods.

of the Almighty, and asked with submissiveness who he himself were? He then answered, 'Were there another than I, I should describe myself through him. I have been from eternity, and shall remain to eternity; I am the first cause of all that exists in the east and west, and north and south, above and below; I am *all*, older than all, the king of kings; I am the truth; I am the spirit of the creation, the Creator himself; I am knowledge, and purity, and light; I am Almighty.'"

These truly sublime ideas cannot fail to convince us, that the Vedas recognize *one only God*, who is Almighty, Infinite, Eternal, Self-existent, the light and the Lord of the universe.

The purely monotheistic period of Brahmaism appears, however, not to have continued more than 1100 years, namely, from 2000 to 900 years before Christ, when a *new commentator* of the Vedas in a great measure altered the contents of the sacred Scripture. This commentator was Menu (Manu), which in fact is only the name of an interlocutor made use of in the work, not that of the author himself, who is unknown.

This work is denominated the Laws (Ordinances, Institutions,) of Menu. It now forms the code of the Hindoos in a spiritual and temporal respect, as the Alkoran does for the Mahometans.

Although the Vedas are referred to by Menu as the basis of the doctrine presented, this doctrine deviates materially from the contents of the original text, and more especially in the following points:—

1. Menu proceeds from other views than those of the Vedas, respecting the *nature of the Almighty* and the *creation of the world.* The Vedas declare that God created the world by the power of his own will. Menu affirms that God and the world are one; that spirit and matter are inseparable; that all is God, and that God is all.*

2. Menu introduces the division of castes as a doctrine of religion, on which subject the Vedas say nothing.

3. Menu introduces the doctrine of the transmigration of souls (metempsychosis), which is not mentioned in the Vedas.

But the Brahmin religion received a still fur-

* We here recognize the basis of Spinoza's substance—pantheism, from which Fichte's idealism and Hegel's ideal-pantheism have developed themselves; all being thus derived from, or agreeing with, the fundamental ideas of the Hindoo philosophy, although subsequently more elaborated by the German philosophers.

ther development by means of the Puranas (a kind of legends, eighteen in number), also regarded as sacred by the Hindoos, which bring the doctrine from the principle of the *unity* to that of the *triad* or *trimurti,* or rather combine the principle of the triad with that of the unity. The *Puranas* moreover introduce the principle of the incarnation, under the name of the doctrine of the *Avatars.*

The Trimurti of the Hindoos seems to have originated in the following manner. The Vedas represent the Almighty as *Creator, Preserver,* and *Destroyer,* and in the last character in respect to the four great periods of the world, or *Yugs,* which, according to the Vedas, are separated from each other by means of great *universal destructions.* From these three attributes the Puranas form three distinct *deities,* under the names of *Brahma* (the Creator), *Vishnou* (the preserver), and *Siva* (the destroyer.)*

* The association in the Deity of the principle of destruction with that of creation, is one of the fundamental ideas of the Brahmin doctrine, and is frequently expressed in their sacred books in a very sublime manner. Thus, for instance, say the Vedas, in their cosmogony: "Numberless are the revolutions in the world, the *creations, destructions,* and *re-creations.* He, the Almighty, brings them forth, as it were, in sport; lets death follow life, and life death."

According to the Puranas, Vishnou and Siva have descended upon earth in a *human form*, as Redeemer, in order to deliver mankind from the ever-increasing power of the evil spirit. These manifestations are called *Avatars*. Of Vishnou they reckon *nine* of them, of Siva *two*, and under each of these they worship the Divine Being.* It

* *Chateaubriand*, in his work entitled *Génie du Christianisme* (vol. v., p. 10), has the following passage: "Le Père Bouchet (a Jesuit missionary in India) a dans sa lettre à l'évêque *d'Avranches* donné les détails les plus curieux sur *le rapport des fables Indiennes avec les principales vérités de notre réligion, et les traditions de l'écriture.*" In page 33, *Chateaubriand* cites *Father Bouchet's* own words, which are as follow: "Je commence par l'idée confuse que les Indiens *conservent* encore de l'adorable Trinité. Je vous ai parlé, monseigneur (the Bishop of Avranches), des trois principaux Dieux des Indiens, *Brahma, Vishnou*, et *Rudren*. (*Ruder*, not Rudren, is one of the many names which the Hindoos give to the third person of the Trinity, *Siva.*)

"La plupart des gentils disent à la vérité, que ce sont trois divinités différentes et effectivement séparées; mais plusieurs hommes spirituels assurent que ces trois Dieux séparés en apparence ne font réellement *qu'un seul Dieu;* que ce Dieu s'appelle *Brahma*, lorsqu'il *crée*, et qu'il exerce sa toute-puissance; qu'il s'appelle *Vishnou*, lorsqu'il *conserve* les être créés, et qu'il donne des marques de sa bonté; et qu'enfin il prend le nom de *Rudren* (Siva), lorsqu'il *detruit* les villes, qu'il châtie les coupables, et qu'il fait sentir les effets de sa juste colère."

"Les *fables* des Indiens ont encore plus de part dans ce qui regarde le *Mystère de l'incarnation;* tous les Indiens conviennent, que Dieu s'est *incarné plusieurs fois*. Presque tous s'accordent

is in this way that Monotheism has been transformed in India, first into the doctrine of the *Trimurti*, and afterwards, by the addition of a multitude of other gods, into a complete *polytheistic* creed.

The Brahmin doctrine is now divided into several branches, each of which has many subdivisions.

The following are the principal branches:—

1st. Vedantism, so named after the Vedanta of Viasa. It has few adherents, consisting of some philosophical Brahmins, such as *Ram-Mohun-Roy*.* Of the thousands of temples in India, there is only *one* consecrated to this doctrine, in which *Brahma* is worshipped *alone*.

à attribuer les incarnations à Vishnou, le second Dieu de leur *Trinité;* et jamais ce Dieu s'est incarné selon eux, qu'en qualité de *sauveur* et de *libérateur* des hommes."

What Chateaubriand subsequently states of the religion of the Hindoos is full of errors, and betrays an ignorance of the subject so much the more unpardonable, since the works of Sir William Jones, as well as those of Colebrooke, were published long before Chateaubriand's *Génie du Christianisme.*

* *Ram-Mohun-Roy* made the most lasting impression upon every one acquainted with him, by his noble appearance, his dignified behaviour, and his prudent discourse. He came to London in 1831, and died there in 1836. He was a perfect master of the English language, as well as of the Sanscrit, Persian, Hindostanee, and Bengalee.

2nd. *Vishnouism.* This doctrine raises the second person of the Hindoo Trimurti (*Vishnou*) to the highest place, and adores his different *Avatars,* together with a multitude of other deities, powers of nature, and mythical persons. Its professors are called *Vaishnadas,* and amount to more than 100 millions. They have temples throughout every part of India, and Brahmins and *Bayaderes** who minister in them.

The *Vaishnadas* fall into two principal divisions. One of them adores *Rama* in the first place, as the seventh of the incarnations of Vishnou; the other, *Krischna* the eighth of these incarnations. *Rama* was a royal prince of Oude, who conquered a great part of India, and even the island of Ceylon. *Krischna* was a prince of the royal family in Mathra, on the river Jumna, and extended his conquests to the west, even to *Guzerat,* where he founded a kingdom. Their exploits are celebrated in the great epic poems, *Ramajana* and *Mahab-harata.*

Both Rama and Krischna were without doubt *historical personages,* who have been exalted to

* They are brought up for the temple service, and receive a more careful education than the Hindoo women in general.

avatars by the Hindoo legend. Rama is a hero of little interest; Hunaman, his counsellor, of somewhat more, although half a monkey and but half a man. Krischna, on the contrary, is represented beautiful and eloquent as Apollo, strong and valiant as Mars, joyful and voluptuous as Bacchus, marching at the head of his army, as formerly the god of wine did, and surrounded by intoxicated satyrs and dancing Bacchantes. But how sensual, how gross, is this representation of an *avatar* of the Deity, a *mediator* and *redeemer!* How infinitely remote from the *one true* and *holy* doctrine, in which *self-denial* is opposed to *sensuality*; *love of mankind*, to the *destructions of the warrior*; and the *sorrow of the cross*, to the *shout of triumphal procession!* Although the *external form* exhibits a deceptive resemblance, yet their *inward spirit* is as different as night from day.

3rd. *Sivaism.* It places the *third* person (Siva) of the Hindoo Trimurti highest in the rank of the gods. The professors of this doctrine call themselves *Saivas*, and their number amounts to many millions. Although Siva is the god of *destruction*, he is also the god of *production*, considered with respect to the idea which ever pervades the doctrine of Brahma, namely, that *death is but the re-commencement of a renewed life.* Therefore Siva is also worshipped under the symbols of procreation, the *Lingam* and *Yoni,** symbols to be found in all the temples of Siva. The priestesses of these temples, like the vestal virgins in ancient Rome, take a *vow of chastity*, the violation of which is punished with death; a severity the more remarkable, as the priestesses of the other gods are *Bayaderes,* with a very different vocation, that of sacrificing to sensual love, for the profit of their temples! How great are the inconsistencies of the human mind! while *virtue, decorum*, and *chastity* are presented as *offerings* in the one temple, the least deviation therefrom is punished with death in the other; and this is the temple of *Lingam!* .

We have seen how the monotheistic principle of Brahmaism, has degenerated to a polytheism, which was still to be increased by the aid of

* *Lingam* is also the symbol of the creating sun, and *Yoni* that of the receptive earth. This *dualism* became the mother of the *trialism* in one of the *Buddhist* sects, when, to the two foregoing principles of creation, the *product* (Buddha) was added.

poetry; the *heroes* who had distinguished themselves by *courage, virtue,* or *beneficence,* were deified by the poets of India, as *Bacchus, Hercules,* and *Saturn* formerly were by the poets of Greece. Goddesses were added as consorts of the gods, personified *powers of nature, elements, heavenly bodies, rivers, fountains, trees, &c.,* by which means the Hindoo Olympus has so increased that the number of the gods can no longer be calculated. The more enlightened, especially the Brahmins, do not share this idolatry, but still support superstition on moral grounds. Human *reason,* they say, immersed in meditation on the Divine Being, grows weary of a way on which it cannot reach the goal. To give but a metaphysical deity to men immersed in sensual objects, is to make them *atheists,*—is to make them miserable.

The *bulk* of the people will neither be satisfied with, nor can they be guided by, a deity conceivable only in thought; they require objects which may be contemplated by the senses, and by means of these they gain a calmness of conviction, and a *peace* in their conduct, which weigh more in the scale of life than all that philosophy has to offer.

How far the Hindoos have lost by the adoption of this principle, is a question which does not belong here; but this is certain, that if, in any country, the *rational* doctrine of the progressive school should spread itself so as to descend into the *cottage, the angel would flee away who brings consolation therein.*

The first want of man is *faith;* but few are capable of raising themselves above the *simple faith* to the *speculative;* bodily toils, daily occupations, and worldly delights prevent them; the mass remains within the narrow circle of the former; nor is it on that account to be pitied, for what it loses in *expansiveness* it gains in *intensity* of faith. Our knowledge is in all cases so small, that somewhat more or less is of little import; it is therefore perhaps best not to investigate what is impenetrable, and to pass the few remaining days in tranquillity, until the soul, freed from its earthly tenement, elevates itself to the fountain of truth, where it shall find the *light,* and see the problem solved which unites *faith* and *knowledge.*

Maimonides, Leibnitz, Kant, Schleiermacher, Schelling, and many others, have endeavoured to combine rationalism with supernaturalism, philosophy with theology, but in vain. The natural cannot be combined with the supernatural.* Let *philosophy* soar into the remotest etherial regions; it does honour to the intellectual power of man. May *religion* remain on earth in her simple white garment,—she brings peace, philosophy does not.

May philosophy speak its own language, *hieroglyphically*; may the language of religion be clear, practical, popular; not high-flown, but eloquent by its *simplicity*; thus has the teacher taught.

* The logical Spinoza expresses himself in the following manner, in his *theologico-political treatise*, cap. 15. "*Theology is neither subject to reason, nor reason to theology*: they who know not how to separate philosophy from theology, dispute whether Revelation (the Bible) should be subordinate to philosophy, or the contrary; that is to say, whether the sense of Scripture should be in conformity with reason, or reason agreeable to Scripture. The latter is assumed by the Sceptics, who deny the sufficiency of reason; and the former by the Dogmatists. It follows, from what has been said, that both greatly err; for whichsoever of these opinions we adopt, we must necessarily do violence either to reason or to Scripture. I have shown that Scripture does not teach philosophy, but only godliness, and that its whole contents are adapted to the capacity of the people. He, therefore, who will judge of Scripture from a philosophical point of

In this way both may contribute to the happiness of mankind, the one by enlarging its horizon, the other by augmenting its peace of mind. In proportion as man advances in knowledge, philosophy opens an extensive field to his exploring eye, and he can then endure the stronger light; the uneducated cannot; he is blinded by it, and falls a prey to his doubts.

But what is your meaning, it will be asked? Will you divide Christians into two classes, of *enlightened* and *unenlightened*, of *sceptics* and *credulous*, of *deceivers* and *deceived?* No! We wish every man to attain the light of truth; we wish that the divine doctrine of religion may find admission into every breast; that all may be equally enlightened, equally virtuous, and equally religious. But when can this be? May it take place in the millennial kingdom! We know that mankind is divided into *educated* and *uneducated*, as well as into rich and poor; into *talented*

view, must attribute to the prophets much that they never thought of, and give a false interpretation to their meaning. On the other hand, he who makes philosophy subject to religion, must allow the prejudices of the bulk of the people in former times to be regarded as divine things, and suffer himself to be deceived by them. Both of them, therefore, the one with *reason* and the other without *reason*, will bring forth absurdities."

and *untalented*, as well as into great and small. May philosophy, therefore, be that *treasure of the temple which may not be lavished on the multitude in its outer court.**

Moreover there is so much *true philosophy in Christianity*, that no one is a loser by keeping to Christianity alone.

The expositions of the Brahmins on their sacred writings are chiefly directed to give instruction in that part of them which relates to the *transmigration of souls*,—a doctrine which gives a peculiar character to the whole earthly conduct of the Hindoo nation. If the doctrine of a *future* spiritual life of reward or punishment forms a powerful restraint for the mind of man, how much more powerful must not that doctrine be, which says, that there is a future *earthly* life of happiness, power, and wealth, which rewards for virtues practised in this life; and a future earthly life of unhappiness, oppression, and poverty, which

* *Our* view is grounded on *facts*, namely: 1st, that philosophy *exists*, and cannot be stifled; 2nd, that the bulk of mankind cannot understand it, and by *immature* apprehension of it would be rendered miserable. The view which will combine both, proceeds from *piis desideriis;* it is beautiful in *theory*, but not *practical.*

punishes for faults committed; so that in this manner the present and the future are connected in one unbroken chain, which, though forged by error, must be as strong as death.

It is to this doctrine that we must ascribe those moral phenomena of daily occurrence in India, which excite the *admiration* or *abhorrence* of the European spectator. With trembling he beholds the young widow, and not unfrequently of an aged husband, whom she scarcely knows and seldom loves, at his death courageously ascend the funeral pile, and burn herself alive.* With astonishment he sees the pilgrim at Jagernaut throw himself under the carriage of the idol, to be crushed to death by its wheels; and with horror he sees, in Rayasthan, a father smother his own daughter, in the hope that she will soon return to the earth, in a happier *male* form.

Yet the father's heart does not beat less warmly in India than in Europe; the Hindoo also loves life too well to sacrifice it beneath the carriage of

* This ancient custom, termed *Suttee*, although strictly prohibited by the British government, is still frequently practised, as also the equally fanatical custom, in some parts of India, of suffocating in milk some of the female children immediately after their birth.

an idol; and the wife longs no more there for the funeral pile than in Europe! What, then, is the cause of this self-denial? The doctrine of the *transmigration of souls*. He who sacrifices himself believes that he will soon return to *this* world in a happier state, as a *reward* for his deed; and indeed the short journey hence and hither again is less gloomy, less perilous than one into the unknown regions of the spiritual world.

According to the doctrine of Brahma the transmigration of the soul is not *inevitable*. By piety, virtue, and a strict obedience to the precepts of religion, the human soul may, without transmigration, immediately attain *Nirvani*,—that is, *happiness*, which, according to the faith of the Hindoos, is a *return to its high origin,—absorption into its divine essence*.

Although steadfast in his faith, the Hindoo is not *fanatical;* he never seeks to make *proselytes*.

If the Creator of the world, he says, had given the preference to a certain religion, this *alone* would have prevailed upon the earth; but as there are many religions, this proves the approbation of them by the Most High. "Men of an enlightened understanding (says the Brahmin) well know that the Supreme has imparted to each nation the doctrine most suitable for it, and he therefore beholds with satisfaction the various ways in which he is worshipped." They regard God as present in the mosques, with those who kneel before the cross, and in the temple where Brahma is worshipped. And is not this faith more in accordance with the *true* doctrine of Christ, than that which lighted the *Auto da fé* for the infallibility of the popes, for the divinity of Mary, and for the miracles of the saints?

What Brahma's doctrine now requires is a *Reformer*, who, like *Luther*, would be able to restore it to its original purity. *Ram-Mohun-Roy* made the attempt, but was unsuccessful; and every one will fail in Asia who does not assume the form of a new *Avatar*.

In its present state the Brahmin doctrine is a confused mixture of *good* and *evil*, of *idealism* and *materialism*, of *superstition* and *libertinism*, of *deism* and *pantheism;* but from this chaos of contending elements, here and there a *flash* of so excellent a nature shoots forth, that it might be deemed an omen of that mild light, which, manifested by the Redeemer, conducts us through the night of life, as the *pillar of fire* once led the sons of Israel to the promised land.*

We know that, "In the beginning, when God created the heaven and the earth, when the earth was without form and void, and darkness was on the face of the deep, and the spirit of God moved on the face of the waters," the naked rock alone rose from the abyss; that after a chaotic night of countless ages a new period of creation began (in the figurative language of the Holy Scripture, a day of creation), which kindled vegetable life, first in the lowest link of the chain, the humble moss, rising in its gradual development to the nobler plants, with the lofty, ever-verdant palm at their head; that after new successive revolutions, organic life began in its lowest link, the zoophyte, when it gradually rose to the crustacea, the amphibia, and the fish; that after renewed convulsions, which raised the bed of the ocean above the clouds, and cast down alps into the abysses of the sea, those monsters of the primæval world arose, which have now happily disappeared, but

* Von allen Religionen, welche in der moralischen und politischen Welt unvertilgbare Spuren zurück liessen, hat Keine so allmächtig wie das Christenthum gesiegt, geherrscht, verwandelt, und gebildet.—*Brinkman's* Philosophische Ansichten.

whose fossil remains furnish irrefragable proofs of their existence; that at a subsequent stage these were replaced by creatures of a higher kind, the mammalia; and that finally, in the last of those periods of creation, the noblest work of the Almighty, man, appeared on the earth, and thoughtfully surveyed the paradise that lay stretched out before him.

But if, in the course of this immeasurable period, there has been a constant development in every succeeding stage, as well of the material as of the organic creation,—if the former has advanced from the naked rock which "at first stood alone in the waters," to those delightful hills, valleys, mountains, and fields covered with noble and luxuriant plants, which now form the riches of the earth; and the latter has risen from the lowest link of organic creation to that glorious image of his Creator, man; may not this development, like a pharos, which in the darkness of night shows the way to the distant harbour, inspire us with the cheering hope, that a similar development may take place in the spiritual world, and that the heavenly guest who animates our perishable clay, will rise higher in every stage of existence, and, drawing nearer to the ideal of perfection, will acquire more and more exalted intellectual power, the noblest of all enjoyments, that which is truly paradisiacal, and after having, in an ethereal form more suited to its mental development, traversed, perhaps, the boundless realms of the universe, and those planetary systems which are the abode of beings more highly organized than we are, at length attain supreme bliss,—absorption into its Divine source. This is the belief of the Brahmin.

THE PHILOSOPHICAL SYSTEMS OF THE HINDOOS.

We must now cast a glance at the philosophical systems appertaining to the Brahmin religion, and of which several are considered *orthodox.*

These systems may be divided into six different classes, under the following appellations:—

1. The elder Minansa, founded by Jaimani.
2. The younger Minansa, or Vedanta, composed by Viasa.
3. The logical school, called Niyaya, founded by Gotama.
4. The Atomic theory, established by Canade.
5. The Atheistic school, established by Capila.
6. The Theistic school, founded by Pantanjali.

The last two are rather Pantheistic systems than Atheistic or Theistic, and are called Sankia. They suppose that *God* and the *world* are the same; that *spirit* and *matter* are one; that *God* is *all,* and *all* is *God.*

Justly to develope these systems* is beyond my abilities, as well as the limits of this treatise; I therefore confine myself to give the main features of the most important of them. The Minansa system deserves particularly to be mentioned; it is founded upon the Vedas, but possesses, moreover, rational grounds in its favour.

God, says Viasa, is omniscient and omnipotent, the creator of all things, the preserver and destroyer; creation is the work of his will. He is himself both the cause and origin of the world. When everything is at an end, all is resolved in him. He is the only subsisting and all-comprehensive spirit. The souls of men are portions of his spirit, which proceed from him as sparks from a flame, and afterwards return to him again. The soul, as a portion of the Deity, is infinite, immortal, rational, sensible, and upright. It has also the power of action, although its natural state is rest (quietism). The operations of the soul are directed by God, in conformity with his own predetermined decrees; these, again, take place

* Colebrooke's Essay on the Philosophy of the Hindoos gives the best account of these systems.

through a long train of causes, which extend back almost into infinity.

The soul is enclosed in the body as in a shell, or, more correctly speaking, a series of shells. In the first is the memory, with the five senses. In the second comes reason; in the third life and sensation. These three constitute the supernatural part of the body, and accompany the soul in all its transmigrations. The fourth shell is the visible body. The soul's relation to the body is as follows :—When man is awake, the soul acts and operates in the visible and actual world. In dreaming there is a figurative and imaginary creation. During deep sleep the spirit is enclosed, but not received into the spiritual being. At death it leaves the body, ascends on high, clothes itself in a watery veil, falls as rain to the earth, is imbibed by some plant, passes through it as nourishment, and forms a new being.* When it has finished its transmigration, the length of which is determined by its actions, it obtains its freedom. This freedom is of three kinds; the first

* Is not this in some measure in accordance with our latest discoveries in vegetable and animal chemistry, if we consider only the material part of man?

perfect, when the soul resumes its union with Brahma; the second, when it only approaches the habitation of Brahma; and the third, much less perfect, when only in this life we receive some of the attributes of the Deity.

The next of the philosophical systems of India, which deserves to be mentioned, if on no other account, for the number of its adherents, is the so-termed system of *Maja*, or that of *Illusions.*

According to this system, there exists *nothing else in reality but Bhrim*, the great spirit; there is neither land nor sea, neither man nor beast, neither tree nor house; all is *Maja, illusion, deception.* What we *see,* what we *hear,* what we *know,* is only a *dream,* a thinking in sleep, death nothing else but an awakening from this sleep, when the soul returns to its senses.

Is not this view of the world rather the effusion of a *mystic piety* than that of philosophy? Of a piety fixing its sight upon the littleness of created things, and the greatness of the Creator, with so much zeal as to pass over from a *comparative* mode of speech to one that is positive? To distinguish between mysticism and scepticism is often very difficult.

There is an episode in the celebrated poem, Mahab-harata, called Bhagavad-Gita, which characterizes the Maja system. Two hostile armies stand opposite each other in battle-array; the young leader of one army is wanting in resolution as the moment approaches when he is to fight against his relatives and friends, who are on the other side. One of its warriors holds the following discourse to encourage him to the combat:—"What dost thou fear? Thou speakest of friends, of relatives, of men! But know that men, beasts, and stones are all one. What is man to-day may be an *animal* to-morrow—perhaps *grass* the day following. The *principle* is eternal; nothing else. Thou art a Khetry; thy caste is that of war; do thy duty. The battle costs a thousand lives. Well, does not the sun shine as brightly the day after? All is *deception* (maja), all is illusion; nothing exists of that which thou thinkest thou seest. Be unmoved within, and think of nothing but the great original *principle*, which alone exists."

The philosophers of India generally assume the human nature to be *threefold* (Tricotomia), consisting not only of *body* and *soul*, but of *body*, *soul* (φρὴν), and *spirit* (θυμὸς).

Pythagoras and Plato hold the same doctrine; that of Pythagoras being probably derived from India, whither he travelled to complete his philosophical studies. Our sacred Scriptures have an expression to the same purport (1 Thes. v. 23): "The very God of peace sanctify you wholly, that your whole *spirit*, and *soul*, and *body* be preserved blameless," &c.

The Indian philosophers regard, as we have already stated, the soul (φρὴν) as an *emanation* or spark of the Divine essence itself, given to *man*, by means of which he received the power of raising his thoughts to those high etherial regions to which the *beast* cannot elevate itself, and by means of which he possesses the power of expressing them *in speech*, and thus of communicating them to his equals. On the other hand, they regarded the *mind* (θυμὸς) as forming a constituent part, which also appertains to *animals*, although not in the same degree of perfection;* they believed that the mind leaves the body at death; but that

* *Cuvier* assumes, that animals have *instinct* and *understanding* (intelligence), between which attributes he draws a definite boundary. The former only has respect to the satisfying of the natural wants or the propagation of the species, and is equally marked in the animals of a lower as well as in those of

in the form of a shadow (umbra) it is able to remain upon earth, hovering around those whom it had loved, and capable of warning and protecting them.

This doctrine is somewhat more consolatory than that of *pantheism,* according to which the soul's *individual* existence is resolved into the vast *universe* of the all-pervading spirit; but is infinitely

a higher organization. Among the more perfect animals, such as monkeys, beasts of prey, ruminating animals, &c., there are evident indications of *intelligence;* it is *instinct* that impels the beaver and the bee to build, the bird to migrate, the new-born child to feel for the mother's breast; but it is *intelligence* that teaches the wolf and the fox to avoid snares, and the domestic animal to distinguish between its fosterer and other persons. Those faculties in animals, which depend on instinct, cannot be changed or cultivated; those which depend upon the intelligence may be improved, not only in the individual but also in the species. Between the animal and human intelligence Cuvier places *consciousness* as a limit; the animal can think, know, remember; but cannot know that it thinks, &c.

But intelligence cannot be found without *mind,* cannot be the *attribute of matter.* Cuvier distinguishes between tamed animals (apprivoisés) and domestic animals (domestiques). Both these kinds require *intelligence;* for taming must be effected by a succession of experiences in the animal, both of the superiority of the man, and of his kindness towards it. Only those animals can become domestic, which, like man, have the instinct to live in society, under the direction of the strongest or oldest. Cuvier supposes that domestic animals merely see in man a leader of the herd.

inferior to that soothing doctrine, agreeably to which man reposes in the bosom of his Divine Creator, as a child in the arms of his mother, in order that he may awake the day after *surrounded by all he holds most dear.*

We might be able to resign ourselves with patient submission to the comfortless doctrine of Pantheism, if it only concerned ourselves; but, together with the hope of our own continued existence, to lose at the same time that of seeing again those whom we have most loved upon earth, to break with them *for ever*, is a reflection that bruises the heart. What! shall we first be bereaved of these beloved ones, retain nothing of them but *memory's* faint shadow, and then, when we are called to follow them, shall even this shadow *fly away from us?* No; such can never be the intention of the *All-bountiful* Creator; he has not deposited in our hearts the tender feelings of love and of friendship, in order at life's goal to rend asunder for ever the band that has been tied by them! They are of a *spiritual* nature; they follow the spirit beyond the boundary of life, where we shall find again those we have loved.

THE EPIC POETRY OF THE HINDOOS, AS A PART OF THEIR RELIGION.

POETRY rules over all in India; it has lent its forms, its colouring, and its charms even to the most abstract sciences, yea, even to *religion*, which has not been a gainer thereby.

The sacred poems of the Hindoos celebrate Brahma, Vishnou, Siva, Brahmanda, Linga, Indra, Vamana, Skandi, Agni, and the rest of their deities; but they more especially celebrate Rama and Krischna as the *avatars* or *incarnations* of Vishnou, the second person of the Deity.

Of the epic poems regarded as sacred, the Ramajana and Mahab-harata are the most remarkable.

The former of these poems celebrates Rama's expedition to the southern parts of India, together with the taking of the island of Ceylon, then called Lanka. Rama was a royal prince of Oude, whose beautiful consort (Sita) was carried off (like the Grecian Helen) by Ravenna, a giant, and king of Deccan. Hanuman, half a man and half a monkey, the leader of an army of the same species (probably Mongolians, or natives of Thibet, whose singular features together with their dress, which was of skins, may have given occasion to this comparison), is more particularly the hero in this piece who contributes to Rama's victories over Ravenna. The name of the poet is Valmiki; the age of the poem nearly the same as that of the Vedanta, 2000 years before Christ.

In the introduction to this poem Brahma utters the following prophetic words:—"So long as the mountains stand, and the rivers flow, *Ramayana* shall live among men." The experience of nearly forty centuries seems to confirm the words of the seer.

The other epic poem, the Mahab-harata, celebrates Krischna's expedition against the tyrant Ravenna, who with his giants stormed the kingdom of the God Indra, called Swerga.* This myth is probably the foundation of the ancient Greek

* See Coleman's Mythology of the Hindus, p. 123, of the ninth Edition.

tradition of the attempt of the Titans to storm heaven.

Among other remarkable particulars in this Poem, is the pure light in which it sets the noble character and high-minded devotion of the women of India, and it shows that we have no correct notion of their state, at least not in *ancient times*. High religious sentiments and a pure morality prevailed then in the East; but this part of the world, like the rest, has had its golden age and its decline. To judge of it from the latter, would be as unjust as to judge the Romish nation during the Republic, to be what it became under the dominion of the popes.

Menu's laws say: "Wives must be esteemed and honoured by their fathers, brothers, husbands, and fathers-in-law, if the latter wish to be happy. The gods rejoice when the wife is honoured; where this is not the case, the sacrifices are unprofitable. When the wife is injured, the whole family decays; when the contrary is the case, it always flourishes."

In the Mahab-harata King Duschmanta utters the following beautiful words:—"The wife is the honour of the family; she who presents the children. The wife is the man's vital spirit, is the man's half, is his best friend, and the source of all his felicity. The wife, with her endearing discourse, is the friend in solitude, the mother to the oppressed, and a refreshment on the journey in the wilderness of life."—See Digest of Hindu law, translated by Colebrooke, *3rd book, s.* 55.

Such exalted ideas of the sanctity of marriage, and of the mutual duties of man and wife, must have excluded polygamy; and it appears from several passages in the laws of Menu, that they prescribe *only one wife*. The fear of dying without offspring may have been the cause of polygamy; for, according to the ideas of the Brahmins, it is the greatest of all misfortunes to depart from this world without having any descendant, who by virtue and pious conduct can obtain for his parents *Nirvani;* that is to say, eternal happiness.

In the Ramayana, paradise is promised to those who marry only *one* wife, and the Hindoo mythology gives no more than *one* to each god.

The heroic poems of India do not exhibit the glowing imagination of the Persic and Arabic productions; but they possess the simple and noble poesy of the Grecian bard. In richness of imagery the Hindoo poetry may vie with that of the Greeks, as the following instance may serve to show: the god of love is called *Kama* in the Hindoo mythology; he is represented as being born of *Makia, seduction,* married to *Retty, desire,* and the friend of *Vassaul, spring.* He is a beautiful but roguish youth, furnished with arrows and a bow of flowers, surrounded by dancing nymphs, and sitting, in the moon's chaste brightness, on a *chattering parrot.* Is not this representation as *poetic* and as *striking* as that of the Greeks? Neither of them, indeed, represent that pure *self-denying* love which lives in its own spirit, offers up all, and desires *nothing* of its object? but this feeling, so rare even in the cold north, how can it be expected under the burning sky of India, in the country where the Bayadere is a priestess! No, *Platonic* love must not be sought there.

The Ramayana and Mahab-harata are not the only poems of great celebrity in India; the Ragtin-vansa, and others, are scarcely less famous, as also the Hitopadesa,* a collection of fables in prose.

* Translated by *A. W. Schlegel* and *Lassen.*

With respect to the *dramatic* literature of the Hindoos, it first became known in Europe from a translation by Sir William Jones of one of its master-pieces, called *Sacontala;* and also by the six dramas subsequently translated by Wilson (printed in Calcutta in 1827, in three vols. 8vo). The *Sacontala* is remarkable both for the beauty of its poetry and for its correct delineation of manners; the author was Kalidas, one of the nine jewels at the court of Vacramadita, contemporary of Augustus Cæsar.

The *Thousand and one Nights,* so universally known in Europe, is a Hindoo original, translated into Persic, and thence into other languages. In Sanscrit the name is *Vrihatkat'ha.**

The literature of India was not studied in Europe before the year 1780, when Sir William Jones prepared the way; and although our progress since has been but small, we can say that it makes us acquainted with a great nation of past ages, which grasped *every branch* of knowledge, and will always occupy a distinguished place in the history of the cultivation of mankind.

* See A. W. Schlegel's work, Etude des Langues Asiatiques.

BUDDHISM.

THE most remarkable feature of *Buddhism* is, not only that it is professed by the greatest portion of the human family, but that it has also extended its doctrines among most of the other religious systems. It is called *Godama's* (Goutama's) doctrine in Assam, Pegu, Ava, and Ceylon; *Samana's* doctrine in Siam; *Amida-Buddha's* in Japan; *Fo's* or *Fohi's* in China and Cochin-China; *Sakiasinka's* in eastern Bengal and Nepaul; *Dherma-Raya's* in Bootan; *A-di-Buddha's* in great Thibet; *Maha-moonie's* * in lesser Thibet; and *Sakiamuna's* in Mongolia and Mantschouri. The total amount of the professors of Buddhism cannot be estimated at less than 380 millions. On adding to these 380 millions of Buddhists, the 150 millions of Brahmins in India, we find that more than half of the human race (calculated in round

* *Maha-moonie*, in Sanscrit, signifies *the great saint*.

numbers at 1000 millions)* profess these two branches of the same fundamental religion.

Buddhism was founded not by *one*, but by several Buddhas, who appeared in India and the neighbouring countries during nine centuries before Christ, and received from its adherents the name of *Buddha*, which signifies *divine man* or *holy man*.

The Brahmins consider the first of these Buddhas (*Sakia*) to have been an *Avatar* of *Vishnou;* a fallen *Avatar*, who preached false doctrines.

The various founders of Buddhism, although differing in their religious principles, agree in the following points:—

1. In acknowledging the Brahmin doctrine as the foundation of their own.

2. In admitting, in conjunction with this doc-

* If the population of the earth be taken at 1,000,000,000, we shall find, from authentic statements, that there are of

Christians	230,000,000
Jews	10,000,000
Mahometans	160,000,000
Buddhists	380,000,000
Brahmins	150,000,000
Pagans in Africa and America, &c.	70,000,000
	1,000,000,000

trine, a *divine triad*, which combines the principle of the trinity with that of the unity, although frequently under other *names* than those of the *trimurti* of the Brahmins.

3. In acknowledging the doctrine of the *transmigration of the soul.*

4. In regarding the *soul* as an *emanation* of the *Divine Being*, which, after having accomplished its transmigration, returns to its high origin.

Buddhism differs from Brahmaism in the following particulars:—

1. It does not acknowledge the Vedas as a revelation from Brahma, but only regards them as a highly deserving human composition, containing great but not revealed truths.

2. It does not recognize the *division of castes*, as does the Brahmin doctrine.*

3. It considers the *inferior gods* and *demi-gods* of the Brahmin religion merely as holy men sent by the Almighty for the benefit of the human race.

These Buddhas, therefore, were (like Luther, Calvin, and Huss) Reformers of religion.

* There are exceptions with regard to this point, as in the island of Ceylon.

The Metaphysics of the Buddhists are distinguished from those of the Brahmins, in that the *God* of the latter pervades and animates the whole of nature, whilst the God of the Buddhists, like that of the *Epicureans, reposes* in a perfect *quietism,* and does not concern himself about human affairs, which, when they have once received their *impulse,* go on in an even course, without his interference. The *God* of the Buddhists does not estimate the value of human actions, and neither rewards nor punishes them! The Buddhists, however, consider what is good to be derived from *virtue,* what is evil from *vice,* and to bring with them temporal *rewards,* or temporal *punishments.* As nevertheless the human mind must have an object on which it can place its hopes, and to which it may address its prayers, they teach that men of extraordinary piety and self-denial, have from time to time appeared upon earth, and in consequence of their distinguished worth, have, after death, been removed to a state of greater happiness, which, however, is but *an absence of all sorrow,* or *suffering,* as health is but the absence of all sickness. These persons, removed at death to bliss, are the

Buddhas, who, next to the *Divine triads*, constitute the object of their worship.

The Buddhists of Ceylon say, that the number of Buddhas is now twenty-two, and that several others are expected on earth.*

According to other Buddhist sects, it is the same Buddha, who at different times, in various countries, and under different human forms, has come upon earth, always as a *saviour* and *redeemer* of the sinful human race.

Some Buddhist sects believe that Buddha returns to the earth every thousand years, and they regard those colossal figures cut out of the mountains, in the neighbourhood of *Bamean* (Hindu Kosch), and in the vale of the upper Indus, as representing some coming Buddha.

The most celebrated Buddhas are, *Sakia*,† *Godama*, and *Fo* (Fud'h-Budd'h). *Sakia* was born to the east of the Ganges, on the confines of *Nepaul*, in a town called *Kapita-Vastu*;‡ *Godama*

* See Coleman's Mythology of the Hindus.

† There are two *Sakia Buddhas*, the one called *Sakia-Muni*, the other *Sakia-Sinha*.

‡ See Wilson's Treatise in the Journal of the Royal Asiatic Society, for the year 1839, 123–160.

was born in *Siam*;* *Fo* was born in the west of India, but the place is unknown.

With regard to the *time* when these Buddhas lived, the accounts differ very much. The chronicle of *Cashmere* says, that it was 1300 years B.C., when the first Buddha lived. The chronicles of the Chinese, Mongolians, and Japanese, assert that it was 1000 years, the Burmese (Ava and Siam), and the Cingalese, that it was 600 years, and that of Thibet, which appear to be the most certain,† that it was 400 years before Christ. But as these chronological computations have respect to *different Buddhas*, they may all be more or less correct.

It appears that the best guide is to consider the eldest *Buddha*, the *Reformer* of the Brahmin *division of caste*, as being younger than *Menu's Codex*, since the latter in fact established the *division of caste* as a *law* (though it might be older as a custom); and as this codex, as I have already shown, is 900 years prior to our compu-

* The Buddhist scriptures of *Ceylon* say that *Godama* was born in that island 623 years B.C., and declared to be Buddha at the age of 35 years, viz. the year 588 B.C.

† *Asoca* held a great Buddhist church-council in Thibet, 110 years after *Sakia's* death, which, according to authentic data, took place 300 years before the birth of Christ.

tation, the most ancient or first Buddha must consequently have been subsequent to this period. Sakia-Sinha seems to have been the eldest Buddha.

The legend of *Godama Buddha* is as follows:*—

A virgin, inspired by heaven, wandered into the wilderness, became pregnant there by a sun-beam, and, although a maid, brought forth a son. Being unable to give suck, a Lotus flower came to her floating upon the water, opened itself, received the tender child, and suckled it. The mother, absorbed in meditation, was conducted by angels to heaven. A holy hermit took the child from the bosom of the flower,† and fled with it to *Camboya*, where it obtained the name of *Godama*. At twelve years of age Godama performed miracles, returned to *Siam*, preached the new doctrine, and was called or regarded as a *Buddha*. Godama is the Buddha worshipped in Ceylon, where he has left the mark of his foot on a rock (called Pik Adam), which now bears a temple dedicated to him.‡

* See the Jesuit Missionary Tachard's account of *Ava*, *Pegu*, and *Siam*.

† Nymphæa Lotos, on this account sacred in India.

‡ These footsteps are called *Phrabat*, and are regarded by

Fo (Fud'h-Budd'h), who founded Buddhism in China, whence it spread to Cochin-China, Tartary, Corea, and Japan, is the youngest of these Buddhas, and came to China under the reign of *Ming-ty,* of the *Ham* dynasty, about the time of the birth of Christ.

That Buddhism continued more than 1000 years in the west of the Indian Peninsula, where also it took its rise, has lately been proved by a Chinese book of travels, translated by *Rémusat,* and commented upon by *Klaproth* and *Wilson.**

The traveller, whose name was *Fo-Hian,* born in the year 399 of our computation, during the reign of *Yao-Hong,* was a Buddhist monk, who travelled at about forty years of age, for the purpose of visiting those places in India, which are considered sacred by that religion; consequently he travelled about the year 440. In his time

the Buddhists in the same sense as the *rainbow* in the religions grounded on the Mosaic records, namely, as an assurance that the deluge will not return. Six such *Phrabat* are found in the East, one of them, singularly enough, in *Mecca,* whither the Buddhists made pilgrimages, long before the rise of *Islamism* in that part.

* See the Transactions of the Asiatic Society for the year 1839.

Buddhism still flourished in many parts of India, and extended from the *Indus* to the *Nerbudda*, but mostly to the east of the Ganges. The persecutions of the Brahmins against the Buddhists had commenced many centuries before, but now increased more and more, until the Brahmin *Kumarilla Bhata* succeeded, by means of a general warfare against the apostate sects, in driving them entirely from *Hindostan*. This took place in the sixth century after Christ, and it is particularly at this period that Buddhism spread over the world, where however it had *long before taken deep root* under different denominations.

That the true seat of Buddhism in ancient times, was Hindostan, is attested by the temples of *Ellora, Elephanta* and *Adjunta*, of which the greater part were dedicated to Buddha, and also by the most authentic Hindoo records.

The Buddhists are divided into two main branches, each of which has its subdivisions; the first is based on *theistic*, the second on *atheistic* principles, or, more correctly speaking on *pantheistic* principles.

The scriptures of the *theistic* branch, are in general written in *Sanscrit*. Those of the *pan-*

theistic are in the *Pali* language, but probably translated from the Sanscrit, in the fourth century of our era. The last-named branch has extended to Thibet, China, Tartary, Ceylon, and in the Indian peninsula to the east of the Ganges, and has about three hundred and fifty million professors. The other branch (the theistic) has its seat in Nepaul, Java, and some of the islands of the Indian archipelago. Its professors are few in number compared with those of the pantheistic branch.

Buddhism, to characterize it in a few words, is a monastic asceticism in morals, and a philosophical scepticism in religion. It divides itself into a multitude of systems, changing in different modes the Brahmaism which is the foundation of all of them; thus, in one of its systems called *Sangata* (which flourishes in Nepaul), it transforms the Brahmin Trimurti, from the names of Brahma, Vishnou, and Siva, into those of A-di-Buddha, Dharma (the feminine), and Sangha, but maintains the same attributes of *Creator, preserver* and *destroyer;* and the same *symbolic* character, of *procreation, conception*, and *production,* though it perplexes, by the change of names, the original Brahmin Trimurti. The *Sanghata system* gives its *triad* the following exposition:—

1. *A-di-Buddha.* 2. *Dharma.* 3. *Sangha.*
1. *Sangha.* 2. *A-di-Buddha.* 3. *Dharma.*
1. *A-di-Buddha.* 2. *Dharma.* 3. *Sangha.*

A-di-Buddha is the creator; *Dharma* the progenitrix; and *Sangha* the production.

The system of Joinville and some other Orientalists, which makes Buddhism more ancient than Brahmaism is entirely groundless, and confuted by the best Hindoo, as well as by the best European *authorities.** Buddhism has assumed different forms in every country, like the reformed doctrines of Christianity. Thus, for instance, in Thibet, it has obtained a distinct character, by means of its *spiritual head,*

* William von Humboldt expresses himself in the following manner (see his remarkable work "*über die Kawi Sprache*," vol. i. p. 290):—"Dass der Buddhismus in Indien selbst, in dem mittleren, an den Ufern des Ganges gelegenen Ländern entstanden ist, und dass er sich erst von dem Brahmanismus, in der inneren Lehre durch die Verwerfung der Veda's, in der äusseren durch die der Kasteneintheilung, trennte, ist nach dem hentigen Stande dieser Forschungen länger keinem Zweifel unterworfen. Sowohl die Annahme eines Vor-Brahmanischen, als eines ursprünglich Ausser-Indischen Buddhismus bedarf keiner Widerlegung mehr."

Dalay-Lama, found there, and who is considered to be *immortal,* so far as the *spirit* of the one *Dalay-Lama* shall successively pass over to the next.*

The best accounts we possess of the nature of Buddhism in Thibet, are by Turner, Bogle, the Russian Archimandrite Hyacinthe Bitschourin, who translated a Chinese work on this subject; and by Schmidt, in the transactions of the Academy of St. Petersburg.

Bogle and Turner were envoys to Thibet, and personally known, the former to Dalay-Lama in *H'Lassa,* and the latter to the Lama in Teschoo.†

* *Turner's* work contains an official letter from the then existing *Dalay-Lama* to the Governor-General Hastings, in the East Indies, in which Dalay-Lama describes his predilection for Bengal, on account of his having been born there twice, during his former abodes upon earth, which had not happened to him in any other land; he therefore sends a considerable sum of money for the purpose of building a temple on the shores of the Ganges.

† Dalay-Lama resides in *H'Lassa,* which is for the Buddhists what Rome is for Catholics. The Lama succession takes place in the following manner: every Dalay-Lama leaves behind him a sealed testament, in which his successor (namely, the person into whom his spirit purposes to pass over) is designated, not by *name,* but by a description of his family (always another than that of Dalay-Lama himself), appearance, age, (most frequently that of a child), and the place where he is to be found. On Dalay-Lama's decease (transmigration), the testament is opened by the *Kuthuktus* (*Cardinals*) assembled in solemn council. The person designated is sought for and pro-

In a conversation with Bogle, Dalay-Lama stated that Brahma, Vishnou, and Siva, were worshipped by the inhabitants of Thibet, but that the lesser gods of India were not otherwise regarded by them than as holy men (Buddhism); that the people of Thibet, from 700 to 800 years back, possessed many temples in India, but that the Brahmins had destroyed them; that India was the real native seat of their gods and their doctrines; and he therefore begged the English envoy to obtain permission from the Governor-General that they might again erect temples on the shores of the Ganges.

The statements of the Archimandrite Hyacinthe also demonstrate that the religion of Dalay-Lama is pure Buddhism; and that this religion, if we except some Tartaric tribes who have gone over to Mahometanism, universally prevails in the high land of Central Asia.*

claimed Dalay-Lama, to whom the people of Thibet take the oath of homage and allegiance.

Banshin Rimbotsai Lama is the second spiritual head of the Buddhists, who resides in *Djachi Lumbo,* a great monastery not far from *H'Lassa.* This Lama *regenerates* himself after the same manner as Dalay-Lama, and is commonly guardian to Dalay-Dama, when the latter is a minor, as Dalay-Lama is for the Lama in Lumbo when the latter is a minor.

* This question is fully discussed by Schmidt in the above-named transactions.

The Buddhists in Thibet, as well as in China, Mongolia, and Corea, have convents like those of the Catholics, the spiritual fathers of which are dressed like Franciscan monks, and make a vow of *celibacy*. They use tonsure, wear the rosary, sprinkle holy water, and celebrate masses with solemn church music. These resemblances astonished the Jesuit missionaries so much, that one of them, father *Gerbillon*, supposed that Buddhism was derived from *Nestorianism* (an anachronism of at least 500 years); another father, *Grémare*, imagined, on the contrary, that Satan himself had caused this resemblance.

This resemblance is also recognized by more recent authors; by *Horneman*, in his comparison between the Oriental doctrines and the sacred Scriptures; by *Munthe* in his Church History; by *Gatterer*, *Richter*, and others.

The most remarkable feature of Buddhism is, that it is professed by the greatest fraction of the human race, and that it has propagated its doctrines among the religious systems of most other nations.

The close affinity of the Egyptian religion with Brahmaism has already been pointed out; but

Buddhism also has penetrated to the banks of the Nile, of which we have many proofs.

Buddhism, as a younger doctrine, must however have come later into Egypt, and probably not before the dynasty of the Ptolemies.

The so-called *Hermes* scriptures (the name of all sacred writings of the Egyptians) contain metaphysical treatises in the form of dialôgue, between Hermes (spiritual wisdom) and *Thodh,* Bodh, Buddh (earthly wisdom), which throughout exhibit the doctrines of Buddhism; they speak of the *pre-existence* of the soul, of its transmigrations upon earth (metempsychosis), of its *emanation* from the Divine Being, and of its *final return* to its high original.*

There is another early Egyptian writing, which in the translation is called *Pimander's Hermes Trismegistus,* and forms a dialogue between *Pimander* (the highest intelligence) and *Thodt,* (Bodh, Buddh), which developes the metaphysics of the Buddhists touching the *Trinity.*

We have seen how Buddhism has spread first

* The *Hermes* scriptures, although they are considered of great antiquity, are probably not earlier than the third century before the Christian era.

over the two peninsulas of India, and afterwards proceeded to Ethiopia, Egypt, China, Corea, Thibet: it penetrated to Chaldea, Phenicia, Palestine, Colchis,* Greece, Rome, Gaul, and Britain. The Samaritans in Aram were Buddhists,† as also the Essenes in Palestine, at least as to their private doctrine, for outwardly they followed the Mosaic law, and subsequently the precepts of Christianity. The Essenes were divided into *contemplative* and *practical.* The contemplative dwelt in the mountainous regions about Nazareth, and on the shores of the Dead Sea. The practical lived in towns.‡ Both of them afterwards joined the Gnostics of Palestine and Chaldea.§

The Gnostics were also divided into two main sects, each of which had its subdivisions; the one sect, which flourished in Meroë in Ethiopia, was called the *Egyptian*, the other the *Asiatic;* the adherents of the latter were in fact Buddhists, who in a great measure adopted the external

* See *Lindner's* Skythien nach *Herodot.*

† See J. Von Müller's Weltgeschichte.

‡ See Hieronymus and Clemens of Alexandria; also Mosheim, J. von Muller, Lib. IX.; and Gibbon, Lib. XV. and XVI.

§ See *Schmidt,* Verwandtschaft der Gnostisch. Theosophischen Lehren mit dem Buddhismus.

forms of Christianity, because they regarded *Jesus* as a Buddha who had appeared on earth, in accordance with their own tenets. The Egyptian Gnostics, on the contrary, although they also were Christians in name, made a metaphysical distinction between *Jesus* and *Christ*, regarding the former as a mere man, but the latter as the *Holy Spirit*, who was incarnated in the man Jesus, and who after his death would return to his high original. These are the doctrines which were cherished by the Gnostics during the first and second centuries of our era, but afterwards they fell into still worse heresies. Simon Magus belonged to the Egyptian Gnostics.*

The Græco-Roman Olympus appears to be least of all allied to that of the Hindoos, though resemblances are found between them, which are pushed too far by Sir William Jones.

The *Ganisa* of the Hindoos may have been the type of the Roman *Janus*.† They are both represented with two faces, which behold the *past* and the *future*, and the name *Janus* may be derived

* See Origen (adv. Celsum); Mosheim (Eccles. Hist.), and Irenæus and Epiphanius.

† Janus pater,—Janus tuens, divus biceps, biformis.—*Ovidius.*

from that of *Ganisa.* *Surya,* the Hindoo god of light, may have been the pattern of the Grecian *Apollo;* they are both represented with a lyre in the hand, and in a chariot drawn by four white horses. *Bacchus* and *Hercules* may also find their types in the Hindoo Olympus; but the *spirit* of the Greek religion is different from that of the Hindoos, and this is of more importance.

To the remote *Japan,* Buddhism has also extended its wide-spreading arms. A king in Corea so eloquently developed the saving influence of this doctrine to a Mikado,* who reigned at the same time, that the latter, captivated thereby, permitted it to be introduced into Japan. It has since extended to such a degree, that it now has more adherents in Japan than the established religion itself, which is denominated *Sinsyn,* or the *Sintoo* doctrine.† The higher classes, however,

* Mikado is the spiritual head of Japan, whose dynasty now numbers twenty-four centuries. The temporal chief bears the name of *Ziogoon;* the power is however in the hands of a self-elective senate or council of ministers (see *Siebold, Fischer,* &c.).

† The *Sintoo* religion has this peculiarity, that in the first place it worships a *goddess* who is called *Ten-sio dai-zin,* daughter of the sun, and ancestress of Mikado. Can it be from this cause that the image worshipped in the temple is a *mirror?*

are followers of a philosophy founded upon the doctrine of Koong-fu-tsé in China.

Even the Druids in ancient Britain were Buddhists;* they adopted the metempsychosis,† the pre-existence of the soul, and its return to the realms of universal space. They had a *divine triad,* consisting of a creator, preserver, and destroyer, as with the Buddhists. The Druids constituted a sacerdotal order, which reserved to itself alone the interpretation of the mysteries of religion. Their wisdom was so celebrated that Lucan expresses himself in the following terms in his poem called Britain:—"If ever the knowledge of the gods has come down to earth, it is to the Druids of Britain." The Druids propagated their doctrines in Gaul during the time of Cæsar, whence they penetrated in the west to the Celtic tribes in Spain, and in the east to Germany, and the Cimbrian peninsula. The ban (*'heacht*)‡ of

* See the remarkable work of Godfrey Higgins, entitled, 'The Celtic Druids, or an attempt to show that the Druids were the Priests of Oriental Colonies, who emigrated from India.' London, 1824.

† Vide Cæsar, Lib. VI.; and Pliny, Lib. XXII.

‡ The German word, *Acht,* is probably derived from this word.

the Druids was equally terrible with that of the Brahmins; even the king against whom it was fulminated "fell," to use the expression of the Druids, "like grass before the scythe."

The *Druids* of Britain received their doctrine from the *Phenicians,* and through the traffic which this enterprizing people had established with Ireland and the British island.*

The spread of *Buddhism* to the above-mentioned parts of the world was for the most part *anterior* to Christianity; *simultaneous* with the establishment of this creed, *Buddhism* penetrates so far as to the *Altai* mountains in Asia, and the *Scandinavian* Peninsula in Europe.

It came to this part of the world by means of a warrior named *Sigge Fridulfson,* surnamed *Odin* (in the ancient Scandinavian dialect *Whodin; in* is the article which, added to *Whod, Bhodd, Buddh,* makes Whodin—Odin), chief of an Asiatic tribe called Asar.†

This *Odin* introduced a religious creed in Scan-

* Vide Strabo on the Cassiterides islands.

† It seems to be the same tribe which came by *sea* to *Etruria.*

dinavia, founded on Asiatic Buddhism, but strangely corrupted.

Many centuries after *Odin,* this creed was codiciled by the Icelander *Snorre Sturelson,** who, by a singular coincidence, which cannot be accidental, gave the name of *Edda* to this codicil, so very like the name of the Indian holy scripture, the *Veda.*

The immense space of time which elapsed between the composition of the *Vedas* (2500 years B.C.), and the *Edda* (1200 years A.D.), must necessarily have changed their contents. It was natural that the names of the gods should be adapted to the nature of the languages, and the metaphors to the difference of climates; but the groundwork is the same, and they both acknowledge *one Almighty Creator,* and the *immortality of the soul.* In the Vedas, the angel asks:—"Who has created the world?" "*Bhrim,* the Father of all," is the reply. In the Edda, Gangler asks:—"Who is the first among the gods?" "The *Father of all,*" is the reply.

* Snorre Sturelson was born in Hram, in the year 1178, A.D. The prosaic Edda is still more recent, and dated from the thirteenth century.

"Where is god?" asks Gangler, in the Edda, "and what has he performed?" "He lives *evermore*," answers Har; "governs his kingdom, and rules over all things, great and small."

Such also is the reply to the angel in the *Veda*.

Jafnhar adds,—"God has created the heaven, the earth, and all that is in them; he formed man, and gave him a spirit, *which shall live and never pass away, even though the body becomes dust, or be burnt to ashes*."

But could a people so uncultivated as the Scandinavians were at the time of Odin have attained such a degree of metaphysical intelligence, unless it had obtained it from a nation further advanced upon thc path of civilization?

Gangler inquires in the Edda:—"How came the world into existence? What was there before it?" Har answers—(in the Wöluspa): "It was the beginning of time, when there was nothing; no sand, no sea, no cool waves. The earth was not, nor the heavens above; there was a yawning gulf, but no grass."

All these questions are so exceedingly similar to those which the angels make to Brahma, and the answers similar to those of Brahma in the Vedas, that we can scarcely question the derivation of the Edda from the Vedas.

The Brahmins (as well as the Buddhists) admit three persons in their deity,—*Brahma*, the *Creator*; *Vishnou*, the *Preserver*; and *Siva*, the *Destroyer*; just so did the Scandinavians. *Allfader* (Father of all) was the *Creator*, *Fjolner* the *Preserver*, and *Svidrir* the *Destroyer*.*

A common symbol of the Creator among the Hindoos (from whom it passed into Egypt) was the scarabæus or beetle. In Scandinavia, likewise, this insignificant insect was sacred, and bore the name of the god *Thor*, *Thor-bagge*, or *Thor-dyfvel*. The superstition yet remains among the people of several provinces in Sweden,† that whoever finds this insect on its back unable to help itself, and turns it on its feet again, atones for his

* The *Trinity* appears in the Scandinavian mythology under six different forms (vide Finn Magnusens Eddalära). In the younger Edda, it appears under the names *Odin*, *Vile*, and *Ve*; in the prose Edda, under the names *Odin* (the supreme), *Jafnhar* (the equally high), and *Tridi* (the third); in *Gylfes Ginnung*, under the names of *Odin*, *Thor*, and *Balder*,—even under those of *Oden*, *Freya*, and *Balder*. In *Oden's* myth it is connected with the *Unity*, as in the doctrine of the Brahmins.

† Vide Afzelii folksagor.

sins, because Thor (like Vishnou) was the *propitiator* with *Allfader* (Brahma).

In an etymological point of view there are also some remarkable resemblances between the Hindoo and the Scandinavian mythology. *Love* is *Kärlek* in Swedish; the god of love bears the name of *Kärlekeya* in Bengal. The abode (heaven) of the god Indra* is called *Swerga* in the Hindoo mythology; *Swerge* is the Swedish name of Sweden,† and is situated near the north pole. *Skand*,‡ the god of war, reigns there (Scandinavia), and seven steps (zones) lead thither, of which the most northern is named *Thule*,§ the ancient name of Sweden.

The resemblance between the *serpent* of *Midgard*, in the Edda, and the *serpent* of *Vishnou*, in the Veda, is also worthy of remark, both being described as having encircled the world. But what is most deserving of observation is the ac-

* Indra is the god of the firmament.

† In one of the stanzas of the *Mahab-harata*, translated by a Brahmin into English verse, there are the following lines:—

> "And on the mount beneath this beam
> The king of *Swerga's* garden smiles."

‡ See Coleman's Mythology of the Hindus, p. 10.

§ See Houghton's Religious Establishment of Merwar.

cordance between the gates of *Walhall* and the Indian ages of the world, or *yugs*. According to the Edda, Walhall has 540 gates; if this number be multiplied by 800, the number of *Einheriers* who can march out* abreast from each gate, the product will be 432,000, which forms the very elementary number for the so-frequently-named ages of the world, or *yugs*, adopted both in the doctrine of Brahma and Buddha, of which the one now in course will extend to 432,000 years, the three preceding ones corresponding to this number multiplied by two, three, and four.†

Although the Scandinavian myth thus appears to have its origin in Brahmaism, or rather in Buddhism, it has immensely *degenerated* from this doctrine, and presents but the picture of a people yet in a primitive state of nature; whilst

* Five hundred and forty doors I believe to be in Walhall. Eight hundred Einheriers can go out abreast when they are to fight against the Ulfven (the wolf). Here is meant the fatal encounter against *Fenris-Ulfven*, at the end of the world, when Oden, at the head of 432,000 armed Einheriers, takes the field against them.—(See the Edda.)

† 1,728,000 = 4 × 432,000
1,296,600 = 3 × 432,000
864,000 = 2 × 432,000
432,000 = 1 × 432,000

Buddhism bears the marks of a nation already far advanced in civilization. The former celebrates bravery and strength as the highest triumph of humanity; the latter seeks it in the exercise of devotion, self-contemplation, and self-denial. Neither does the Scandinavian myth exhibit the least of that *contemplative metaphysical* character which distinguishes the doctrine of Buddha; it is *rough, warlike,* and *wild,* like the people that professed it; but there is a deep sense in it which betrays its *origin.**

* *Odin* (Sigge Fridulfson) came with his *Asar* from the coasts of the Black Sea; *Cholchis*, on the same sea, was a colony of Buddhists. See *Lindner*, in his work on *Scythia, according to Herodotus*, and *Rennell's* Geography of Herodotus.

THE JAINAS.

THE *Jainas* (Dschainas) are a reformed religious sect from Brahmaism, which adopts the doctrines of Buddhism ; but they are distinguished from the latter by having retained the *division of castes*, on which account they have been allowed to remain in India.

The sect is of great antiquity, as is evident from the fact of many of the most ancient mountain temples having belonged to the Jainas ; they may have separated from the mother-church at the same time with the Buddhists.

The Jainas acknowledge the *Trimurti* of the Brahmin religion, like the Buddhists, but not its other gods—at least not otherwise than as holy men. The Jainas have besides 27 peculiar saints, called *Tirt-hankaras*, whom they regard as *Avatars*, or incarnations of *Vishnou ;* they recognize, moreover, the incarnations of *Siva.*

It is remarkable to observe how the *unity* combined with the *trinity*, for a period of more than

3000 years, forms a fundamental doctrine of the most ancient and most cultivated nations of the world.

It is recognized in the doctrine of Brahma, of Buddha, of the Jainas, among the Egyptians, in Plato, Pythagoras, Parmenides, and among the Celtic Druids; and above all it is found again, on a more sure basis, in the *revealed doctrine of the Christian religion.*

But ought not this accordance in faith of the greatest and most distinguished portion of the human race, during the course of more than 3000 years, respecting a mystery incomprehensible to the feeble understanding of man,—ought it not, I say, to be regarded as a further proof of the sublime truth which lies at its foundation?

The Jainas retain more vividly than the Brahmins themselves, the doctrine of the *transmigration of the soul,* and therefore have the greatest aversion to the killing of any animal. They protect them to such a degree that they even maintain hospitals for the most loathsome kinds.

It is in the north-west of India that the Jainas have settled themselves, though not in great numbers. Their temples are in general larger and more stately than those of the Brahmins, and they are themselves less superstitious than the orthodox Hindoos.

Rishabha is the name of the most revered of their *Tirt-hankars.* He was an *avatar,* and came upon earth thirteen different times. A later *Tirt-hankar* is said to have been incarnate twenty-seven times. Godama (Gutha, Buddha) was, according to the Jainas, only a disciple of this *Tirt-hankar.* Thus it is that each sect exalts its own prophet above the rest.

What has been stated in this and the preceding chapter on the origin, antiquity, and nature of *Buddhism* and the connected *Jainaism,* is in *substance* founded on the authors mentioned below,* who, although opposed to each other in several cases, have left the impression of the correctness *of the general view* taken here of those religions.

* Abel Remusat, Essay sur la Doctrine des Buddhist; Klaproth and Burnouf's articles in the Nouveau Journal Asiatique; those of Colebrook and Wilson in the Transactions of the Royal Asiatic Society; Schmidt's Treatises in the Transactions of the Academy of St. Petersburg; William von Humboldt on the Kawi Dialect; Upham on the *Sangata* Doctrine; Deshauteray sur le Buddhisme en Chine; and Houghton Hodgson's Sketch of Buddhism in Nepaul. Older, but still instruc-

tive sources, are—Coleman's Tigrana; Franklin's Researches on the Doctrine of the Jainas and Buddhists; James Law on Buddha and the Phrabat; several articles in the Asiatic Journal; A. W. Schlegel's Indische Bibliothek; the Oriental Magazine.

Carl Ritter, who is so justly celebrated as a geographer, appears to have been chargeable with *exaggeration*, when, in his learned etymologies, he gives the following statements respecting Buddhism (See Vorhalle der Europæishen Völker Geschichten, pp. 30, 32.)

"Ausser dem Nahmen, finden wir auch den Kultus des *Buddh* oder *Boda* der Inder, durch gang Westasien und den Occident in sehr alter Zeit, unter mancherlei Wechseln, doch in gleichem Wesen verbreitet, als *Goito Syr* der Skythen (Γοιτόσυρος. Herod. IV. 59), nach Herodot der Apollon, nämlich wohl der Hyperboräische; als *Vod-her* der Wenden, *Bogh* der Slaven, *Odin* der Sachsen und Scandinavier, *Wodan* der Germanen, *Khoda* der Perser, *God* der Britten, *Gott* der deutschen Sprache; dagegen nicht aber den des Brahma; dann blosse Namensverwandtschaft wäre zu schwach, ihn in denn Bacchischen Zuge als Bromios (Euripid. Bach., v. 141) oder in Orpheus Brimo wiederfinden zu wollen (Orph. Argon. v. 17). Zugleich treffen wir jenen Namen wieder als einen reliogiösen ganzer Völker seines Kultus, nämlich bey *Budiern* in Medien und *Budinen* in Skythenlande am Oaros an, beyde bei Herodot (Herod. I. 101, IV. 109); ferner bey *Buditiern* und *Bottiäeren* nach Herodot, Thucydides und Strabo (Strabo, ed. Tzsch, VI. p. 287; Herod. VII. 123), in Macedonien, Japygia und am Adria-Meere. Wir finden ihn als die Benennung urältester Götter, Heroen, Heiligthümer, Priestergeschlechter und Landschaften im vorheraklidischen Griechenlande fast überall verbreitet und von grosser Bedentung; so den Heros *Buto* (Bodo) in Dodona als Stifter des ältesten Thessalischen Orakels, das früher *Bodana* hiess (Steph. Byz. ed. Berkel. Fr. p. 235); die *Minerva Budia*, die im alten Thessalien verehrt ward (Lycophron. Cassandra, v. 359); Herakles den *Budonen* (Βουδώνης, Hesych. Alb. p. 757), der durch die Flamme gereinigt zu den

Obern Göttern eingeht. Wir finden ihn in dem Vaterlande Achilles bey Homer, in dem wohlbewohnten *Budeion* (Ilias XVI. 572), in Attika im Tribus Butu-Oenoe bey Eleusis, auf Salamis und anderwärts in alten Festen und Bauten, *Budoron* genannt. Wir finden ihr häufig wieder, zumal auch in dem alten Attischen Heros *Butes* (Pausan. Attic. I. 26) und dessen Priestergeschlechte den *Butaden* und *Eteobutaden*, welche die ältesten Priester der Pallas Athene waren, dem Homer schon bekannt; in den *Botachiden* Arkadiens (Pausan. VIII. 45, und Steph. Byz. ed. Berkel. p. 252), in den *Butakiden* auf Naxos, in Karien, auf Sicilien als Erbaner des Tempels zu Eryx u. s. w. also in weiter Verbreitung im Süden, nach vielen der ältesten Fragmente der griechischen Autoren. Landeinwärts aber, im Germanischen, nördlichern Völkergebiete, ist derselbe Name, mit der älteste, bedeutendste unter allen, die auf uns gekommen, wie schon aus den verschiedenen Namen der Emporien (immer geweihete Stellen) *Budorikum*, *Budorgis* mitten in den Sudeten, *Maro-boduum*, dem Markomannensitze, *Buddissin* der Slaven, *Butinfeld* Wittekinds, diess hervorgeht, wie aus heiligen Wassernamen, im *Boden-See* (Bodungo bey Geogr. Rav. ed. Porch. p. 187), der ein Heiligthum des Wodan war, das erst Sanct Gallus entweihete: im *Bottnischen* Meere (daher Codanus sinus) im fernen Hyperboräerlande und anderwärts, von denen unten weitläuftiger die Rede seyn wird."

THE SHEIKS.

THE Sheiks, or Seiks, form a religious sect which had united into a nation under the former empire of Runjet-Sing. They possess the Punjaub.

Baba Nanuk, a Hindoo of the Khetry caste, was the first founder of the sect; he was born in 1469, and died at 70 years of age, in *Lahore.* He was succeeded by several other *Gurus* or teachers, among whom *Govindu Singh* is the second and most famous founder of the sect.

Baba Nanuk's object was to form into one doctrine Brahmaism and Mahomedanism, but regarding the deities of the Brahmins, more as holy men, sent by God for the amendment of mankind.*

Govindu Singh gave another character to the sect. He rejected both the *Alkoran* and the *Puranas,* but retained the *Vedas* as being of a *monotheistic* nature.

* See Sir John Malcolm's Sketch of the Sikhs, pp. 144, 197.

The sect was almost exterminated by the Afghan Bhadur Shah, Emperor of Delhi, but has again increased during the course of the last century, so that, being now united into a tribe, it holds under different chiefs possession of the said kingdom of *Lahore*.

The chief seat of the Sheik religion is in *Umritzir* (Umritu-Suru), a considerable town in the Punjaub. Its great temple preserves the sacred scripture of the Sheiks (*Grunthu*), composed by *Nanuk* and by *Govindu Singh*. There the chief priest is seen seated upon a throne, holding the sacred book before him, absorbed in contemplation. The people kneel down and make prayers often by night, when the temple is illuminated.* On an altar with gold brocade, lies a *sword* and *shield*, as symbols of the martial spirit of the sect. In the fore court of the temple is a sacred spring called the well of immortality, which, from its magnitude, 300 feet in circumference,† forms a natural phenomenon.

* See Jaquemont's Voyage aux Indes, Tibet, et Cachemire.

† See Baron von Hügel's Kaschmir und das Reich der Seiks, Vol. III. p. 403.

THE MAHOMETAN TRIBES IN INDIA, THE GUEBERS OR PARSES, AND THE SYRIAN CHRISTIANS.

THE *Mahometans* of India, are descended from its former conquerors, the Mongols, Afghans, and Persians, and constitute a population of not less than 15,000,000, so that the queen of England has more Mussulmans under her sceptre than the Grand Sultan himself.

Tamerlane's conquest of Hindostan, and the continuance of his dynasty upon the throne of Delhi for several centuries, has caused a great portion of the princes of India, as well as their courtiers, to become Mussulmans.

The Mussulmans are in general a more moral sect than the adherents of Brahma. The Old Testament is retained in the Alkoran, and Christ himself is considered as a prophet. The great defect of the doctrine, independent of its errors, lies in *polygamy*, which depraves everything, degrades the woman, and forms an inexhaustible source of decay within the closed *Harem*.

The devotion in external form of the Mahometan is greater than that of the Christian, and shows what an influence the prophet has exercised on the minds of his disciples.

The *Guebers* or *Parses* occupy, next to the Mahometans, the first place among the foreign creeds of India. They are a remarkable people, and have, although surrounded by other religions, preserved their doctrine in its purity. They adore the *sun* as an emblem of the Supreme Being, and maintain in their temples the *sacred fire*, as a symbol thereof. Zoroaster was the founder of their religion, and their scripture is the Zend-Avesta. The Parses came from Persia, about 900 years ago, and have spread themselves in the western parts of India; the town of Bombay contains about 10,000 of them. They are distinguished by their fine appearance, their prosperous condition, and their industry. Next to the English, they carry on the greatest trade in India, are excellent ship-builders, belong to the middle classes, and do not pay any attention to agriculture.

Syrian Christians are also found in India, who follow the doctrine preached by the Apostle Thomas. They had formerly upwards of a thousand churches in the western part of India, but were so severely persecuted by the Portuguese, in the seventeenth century, that they have now but a small number left. The priesthood of the Syrian church is *hereditary in those families* to which the Apostle committed the sacred office. They do not recognize the infallibility of the pope, the sanctity of the Virgin, or the images of the saints, and thus approximate to the Protestant church; their ritual is, however, in Latin.

In the Himalaya mountains there is a people, which, though of Hindoo religion, differs from the rest in several particulars; instead of *polygamy*,* they have adopted *polyandrie;* which gives every wife the right to take *several husbands; brothers* are chosen by way of preference.

* Brahmaism, according to the laws of Menu, enjoins but one wife, but permits two concubines, which are kept by the rich only.

This custom is derived from the adjacent country of Thibet, where it has existed for many centuries.*

* See *Conolly's* Journey to the North of India, and *Turner's* Embassy to the Court of the Teshoo Lama.

NATIONS OF INDIA.

The Hindoos may be divided into two great sections, one of which occupies *Hindostan,* the northern part of the Indian peninsula, whilst the other occupies the *Deccan,* which forms the southern part. Those parts are separated from each other by the river *Nerbudda,* and by the *Vindhia* mountains, inhabited by a darker race than the Hindoos, and with a language not of Sanscrit origin.

That portion of the Hindoo nation, which occupies the Hindostan, has the common name of *Ariens,* derived from the Sanscrit word *Arja,* which signifies " good people—obedient to the law." They settled first in Oude, between the Ganges and the Sarja, where the sacred cities of *Ajodhiâ* and *Pratish-shana* were situated.

The people of the *Deccan* are descended from those of Hindostan. Their language is the *Tamul,* which has degenerated more from the Sanscrit, than the different languages of the nations of Hindostan.

The *Ramajana* celebrates the emigration of the people of Arja, to the south of the Vindhian mountains in the Deccan, which at that time was wild and covered with forests. The chief of one of those migrations, Agastia, is mentioned in the poem. The inhabitants whom he found in the mountains of Vindhia are called *Apes,* and play a part in the conquests of Râmâ, of the island of Ceylon (*Lanka*).

The above-mentioned two great sections of the Hindoo people are subdivided into a multitude of others, forming nations which, in character, appearance, and manners, differ from each other much the same as the nations of Europe. We find among them many which are warlike and active, and others who are effeminate and indolent. The nations who inhabit the northern part of India, Rayasthan, the Punjaub, Malwa, Oude, and Rohilcund are warlike, the southern more indolent. In Rayasthan, we may fancy ourselves carried back to the middle ages of Europe, and to the times of feudalism. On the summits of the mountains we find castles with walls and watch-towers not inferior to those whose ruins still adorn the banks of the Rhine, the Loire, and the Danube. There the Raypoot resides, surrounded by his vassals, like the ancient feudal lord in Europe. Mounted on his charger, with helmet, shield, and lance, he carries on the hereditary feud against some hostile neighbour; while his dark-eyed daughter is seen on her Arabian steed, hunts the tiger, or tends the wounded warrior in her father's castle.

To the south of Rayasthan we meet the *Mahrattas*, a martial people, fanatically devoted to their religion, and unwearied defenders of India, a great portion of which they had themselves subdued. With the swiftness of the wind, you see thousands of Mahratta cavalry attack a state, often very distant, lay waste and destroy everything in their way. They say, that the saddle of their Rayah's horse, is his Durbar (throne), and that every land belongs to him, which he can reach with the lances of his soldiers. Still more warlike are the *Pindaries*, properly a band of freebooters, but of such a formidable description that they once possessed upwards of 30,000 cavalry in the field.

As a contrast to these warlike tribes, we find in the south-eastern parts of the peninsula, in *Bengal*, *Circars*, and the *Carnatic*, an effeminate, weak, peaceful people, who toil in their rice-fields, and tend their sugar-canes, without caring who holds the rule in India,—the Mogul, the Mahratt, or the Briton,—provided they can get their harvest in security, and can offer to the images of their gods in peace.

But everything is peculiar, grand, and romantic in India,—from the steel-clad knight of Rayasthan, to the devoted Brahmin in the temples of Benares; from the fierce Mahratt on his fleet and active steed, to the Nabob moving gently on his elephant; from the amazon, who chases the tiger in the jungle, to the Bayadere who offers in *volupté* to her Gods. Nature, too, in this glorious country is chequered with variety, and clad in glowing colours: see the luxuriance of her tropical vegetation, and the hurricane of her monsoons; see the majesty of her snow-covered Himalaya, and the dryness of her deserts; see the immense plains of Hindostan, and the scenery of her lofty mountains; but, above all, see the immense age of her history, and the poetry of her recollections!

How these affect and elevate the human mind, we feel in our own breast. Does not the petty stream where Ilion stood, affect the mind more warmly than the Ohio and the Mississippi? Does not the Roman capitol in its decayed state, inspire a greater interest than the new-built house which bears this name at Washington? Why! the past is the poetry of the heart, the present its often pale and colourless drama, the future the ominous enigma of which the solution is,—in the hand of the Almighty.

COSMOGONY OF THE HINDOOS.

THE sacred writings of the Hindoos contain remarkable accounts of the *creation, and of the inundation of the world.* According to those writings this inundation took place 3000 years before Christ,* which pretty well accords with the computations of our own holy scriptures.

The cosmogony of the Hindoos is contained not alone in the Vedas, and in the *Vedanta,* but also in the codex of *Menu.*

This codex commences, like the books of Moses, with an account of the creation of the world, which is expressed in the following terms:†—

Menu (Manu), absorbed in contemplation, was

* See *Mountstuart Elphinstone's* History of India, vol. I. p. 258.

† We here follow the translation from the Sanscrit which has lately been published by *Loiseleur des Long-Champs.*

surrounded by *Maharchis* (angels), who with humility said to him—

"Lord, thou who alone knowest the original principle (the Creator), self-subsistent, infinite, incomprehensible, and inconceivable to the feeble understanding of man, tell us, who were they who were first created, and who were they who were created afterwards?"

Menu cautiously replied, "The world was sunk in darkness, was invisible, and could not be discovered either by the power of thought or in reality, for it lay sunk in slumber; but when the slumber (pralay-chaos) was at an end, *He* then made the world *visible*, with its five elements, and its other appurtenances; He who created himself, and who cannot be comprehended by our senses.*

"He, shining with the most glorious brightness, dispelled the mist, and developed nature (Pracrita).

"He whom the *spirit* alone can comprehend, but not the faculty of man; He who is invisible,

* The name of the *Creator*, too holy to be pronounced aloud, is *Aum;* it is written A. U. M., which three letters denote the three persons of the Hindoo *Trimurti.*

who is eternal, who is the soul of all beings, then developed all his glory.

"Resolving in his inward thought, from his own substance to create the world, he first made the water, and deposited the seed (germen) therein.

"From this germ arose an egg (fœtus), which, like the sun, shone with a thousand rays; it was in this that the Almighty was brought forth to the world, under the form of *Brahma*, the author of everything living.

"The water was called *Naras,* because it was created by *Nara*, the holy spirit, *who hovered over the water;* and the spirit was called *Narajana*, because he hovered over the water.

"It is the eternal principle (Verbum) which thus created the divine being (Pouroncha), known in the world under the name of Brahma.

"After Brahma had remained one of his years* in the light-beaming egg, he separated it by the power of his will alone, made thereof *heaven* and *earth*, which he divided by *air* and *water*.†"

* One of Brahma's years corresponds to a period of the world (*yug*) of 432,000 solar years.

† That the *Greeks* derived their cosmogony from the Hindoos, may be seen in the account which *Damascius* has given of

The Buddhists have another cosmogony than that of the Brahmins: their sacred writings, *Tantras,* contain the following account of the creation of man:*—

"In the beginning the earth was uninhabited; at which time the inhabitants of heaven, or of *Bhurana* (the angels), used to visit the earth.

"These glorious beings, consisting of *men* and *women,* through the purity of their spirit, had never yet cherished any *sensual desires,* when A. Di Buddha (the supreme God) infused into them the desire to taste the fruit of a tree resembling the almond, which excited the sexual appetite in them, and they afterwards disdained to return to *Bhurana* (heaven), and thus became the parents of the human race.

the doctrine of Orpheus. (Vide Creuzer's Symbolik, Vol. I.) It is as follows:—"In the beginning was *Kronos,* who out of *Chaos* created *Æther* (day), and *Erebos* (night); therein he laid an egg (Hindoo!), from which came *Phanes,* furnished with three heads (the Brahmin Trimurti); *Phanes* created the man and the woman, from whom the human race is derived."

The cosmogony of the Egyptians also adopts the Hindoo egg, which, divided into two, formed heaven and earth. (Vide Diodorus and Plutarch).

* See *Houghton Hodgson's* Letter to *Colebrooke,* on the Cosmogony of the Buddhists of Thibet. Asiatic Society's Journal, Vol. II. part 1, p. 234.

"The first-born man was called *Maha Samvat* (the great first-born); he was king over the whole earth," &c. &c.

The cosmogonies of the other oriental nations are more or less in accordance either with that of the Brahmins or with that of the Buddhists.

Not one of them, however, exhibits such a character of sublimity, truth, and inspiration as the Mosaic cosmogony, which is too well known to require to be repeated here.

Its chronological computations (according to certain genealogical registers) do not, however, agree with those of all other ancient nations; and as these computations do not form any essential part of the contents of the sacred scriptures, we may be allowed, without prejudice to them, to compare its *calculations* with those of some other Asiatic nations.*

This may so much the rather be done, as these computations are even different in the *very text of the Mosaic scriptures:* thus we find, for example,

* The names given in the Mosaic genealogies may possibly be those of entire dynasties or families (as in the Egyptian chronology), and not of *individuals*: if so, it would considerably increase the time alleged.

that the Alexandrine text, differs from the *Masoretical Hebrew* text, by no less than 1376 years in the computation of the time elapsed between the *creation* and the *deluge.**

On comparing the Mosaic chronology with that of other early nations, we shall follow the Alexandrine text as being the most ancient, and that which, by its higher computation of time, best agrees with the chronologies of the other ancient nations.

The Alexandrine version of the Mosaic books reckons a period of 2262 years as separating the *creation* from the *deluge,* and a space of 3138 years as dividing the deluge from the conquest of Egypt by Alexander. If we assume this to have taken place about 350 years before Christ, we shall have a period of 5750 years between the birth of Christ, and the existence of man upon the earth.†

* See J. Müller's Versuch über die Zeitrechnung der Vorwelt.

† According to the Masoretic text, it is not more than 4374 years. *Klaproth* (see Asie Polyglotte) quotes a passage from *Kennicot,* in which that profound Hebraist avows a reluctant conviction, that of the three eldest versions of the Old Testament, the Jewish, the Septuagint, and the Samaritan, the former has been designedly falsified.

But this space of time is infinitely small in comparison with the records of all other Asiatic nations; and these records, if in no other respect, yet, at least, in a *chronological* point of view, are deserving of our attention.

Thus, for example, the *Bactrian* document, called *Dabistan**, gives an entire register of kings, namely, of the *Mahabadernes*, whose first link reigned in *Bactria* (the present *Balk* and *Bamean*) 5600 years before Alexander's expedition to India, and consequently several hundred

It appears that there was a tradition amongst the Jews, that the advent of the Messiah was to take place in the six thousandth year of the world.

It became, therefore, an object of the Jews, to show that the date of our Saviour's ministry was too early for this period of the six thousand years, and an object of the Christians, to prove the contrary. For this purpose the former counted genealogies in such a manner, as to place the *flood* 2348 years before the birth of Christ.

The latter (the Christians) counted between 3000 and 4000 years, namely, the Samaritans 3044, and the Septuagint text, 3716. If we take the Samaritan calculation of 3044 years between Christ and the flood, and take 2262 years between the flood and the creation of man, it gives a period of 5306 between Christ and the creation of man, and an elapsed term of 7150 years to the present year, 1844.

* Found in *Cashmeere*, and brought to Europe by Sir William Jones. According to W. Schlegel, the Dabistan is of *Persian* origin, and of more recent date.

years *before* the time given by the Alexandrine text, for the appearance *of the first man upon the earth.*

So also the *Iran* record gives a whole register of kings, namely, the *Pischdadiernes,* whose founder reigned 5400 years before the expedition of Alexander to India, and who consequently, according to the computation of the Alexandrine text, would have been contemporary with Adam.*

Diodorus mentions a *Turanic* or *Sogdianic* dynasty, that of the *Elohernes,*† who reigned long before the period of the creation, as stated in the Mosaic records.

So also the Chinese document (Schuking) already mentioned, gives registers of kings far more ancient than the *Adamic* period. *Manetho* likewise specifies genealogies of Egyptian kings, which extend 2000 years farther back than the time given by the Alexandrine text for the *period of the creation,* and more

* See J. Müller's Versuch über die Zeitrechnung der Vorwelt.

† This dynasty of twelve kings, which commences with *Helios,* and closes with *Aphroditis,* may possibly be *symbolical,* and denote the twelve signs of the Zodiac.

than 3000 years prior to that of the Masoretic text.*

These comparisons lead to the natural conclusion that we have not *rightly* comprehended the chronology of the Mosaic records, and that the space of time elapsed between the *creation of man* and the *flood,* must have been *much greater* than this document appears to specify.

This conclusion, if well founded, might justify the *attempt* to ascertain, not the time of the creation of man, or the place of his first abode (the *biblical Eden*), which is a mere *theological* question; but the time in which the progenitors of the human race *were congregated to a people, and the geographical place of the abode of this people, may be found on earth.*

In order to ascertain this time and this place, we must first inquire what the *records* of ancient nations relate, respecting the great *deluge* which overflowed the earth, *where* and in what countries men then *existed,* and from *whence they came to these countries.*

The Indian Bhagavat-Purana (in a chapter en-

* *Schlözer* and *Rotteck* on this account do not consider the Egyptians to have been *Noachidæ.*

titled *Matoya Avatar*) expresses itself in the following manner concerning the great flood which overflowed the earth, and whereby the greater part of mankind perished.

"Vishnou," says the Purana, "manifested himself under the form of a little fish, which was continually becoming larger, in order to warn the virtuous king *Sakiavrata** of the great deluge which would destroy everything. Vishnou did this in the following words:—'After seven days,' said he, 'a great flood will take place upon the earth, and destroy everything that exists, together with mankind, on account of their sins; but I will send to thee a *great ship* into which thou shalt bring all useful plants and their seeds; and let seven holy men accompany thee, and take with thee a *pair* of all living animals, in order to save thyself and them, from the general destruction. No other light shall then be found upon earth but the lustre of the holy men who attend thee,'" &c.

This Purana gives an astronomical computation, according to which the great deluge

* He was king in *Dravira*, a state in the southern part of the Deccan.

took place about 3000 years before the birth of Christ.*

The Hindoos maintain that the present period of the world, *Kali-Yug*, commenced at the close of this deluge. The name *Kali-Yug*, with the addition of *Dew* (Dios, Deus), forms the root of the *Deukalion* of the Greeks. The Hindoos, who *personified* everything, represented this period of the world under the form of a *demi-god*, the son of *Pramathesa*, from which the Greeks formed *Prometheus*, whose son was *Deukalion*.

After the Hindoo tradition of the flood, we give that of the *Zend-people's*, contained in their sacred scriptures. The *Zend-Avesta* says that a fire-spitting star (a comet) fell upon the earth and kindled a fire therein, when *Ormuzd* (the good principle, in opposition to *Ahriman*, the evil principle) extinguished the fire by inundating the earth with a great *flood of water*, which destroyed the greater part of the human race.

Bundehesch, the sacred scripture of the ancient Persians (Parsées), contains the same account. It says that *Cayonmortz* and his wife were the only

* See Sir William Jones's Works, Vol. I. page 230.

persons who escaped the great deluge, and that all men now existing are descended from these two.

The most ancient traditions of the *Chinese,* reported in the *Schuking,* state (see De Guignes) that *Jao* (who, according to this chronicle, reigned 2350 years before Christ), by digging canals, carried off the water, which, in consequence of a *great and universal deluge,* caused the low lands, still under his reign, to be uninhabitable. This deluge, according to the same chronicle, is said to have been so terrible, that it rose to the skies.

The *Chaldee* records contain the following account of the great flood which overflowed the earth (see Berosi Chaldæorum Historia, edited by Richter):—Kronos, it says, showed himself in sleep to *Xisuthros,* the king of Chaldea, and informed him that on the fifteenth day of the month *Dæsios** a great flood would destroy everything on earth. Kronos therefore commanded *Xisuthros* to build a vessel *five stadia* in length, and *two*

* We here find the *solar year* divided into months, which supposes a far advanced state of astronomical science at the time when the deluge took place, and of course a considerable progress in *civilization.*

stadia in breadth, upon which he should bring his relations, friends, meat and drink, and all kinds of animals and plants. It says further, that *Xisuthros*, when the flood decreased, sent out some birds, which, as they did not return on the third day, caused him to know that the deluge was at an end. It states that *Xisuthros* rested with his vessel on a mountain called *Korydureus*, where he erected an altar, sacrificed to the gods, and disappeared in a cloud.

Xisuthros (Sesostris), according to *Berosus*, lived 2000 years before him, and as *Berosus* lived 500 years before Christ, the great deluge, from this account, must have occurred 2500 years before Christ.

The chronicle of the Armenians gives the same account of the deluge, and states that it took place 3000 years before Christ. *Josephus* names a town that was built upon the mountain on which the ark rested, and which after this event was called *Nohidchedan*.

The Grecian mythology relates how *Deukalion*, king of Pythia, was informed by *Zeus* of the great flood which should destroy the human race. It states that *Zeus* ordered him to build a vessel of cedar-wood, in which he might save himself and his family, and that the vessel rested on mount *Parnassus*, which, according to the calculation of *Hoserius*, took place 2500 years before the birth of Christ.

Ogyges (a second Grecian Noah), according to *Varro*, lived 2540 years before Christ. The account of this flood agrees with that of *Deukalion*.

Apollodorus mentions the vessel in which *Deukalion* was saved, and also the doves which were let out, in order to ascertain if the flood had abated.

There is still to be found in the hall of the propyleum tower at *Karnak* (Egypt) a painted representation of the *ark*.

Diodorus mentions the model of an *ark*, 280 cubits long, of cedar, overlaid with gold, and dedicated by *Sesostris* to the Temple of Ammon at Thebes.

Plato makes mention of the great deluge (in Timæus), and refers the destruction of *Atlantis* to this event.

The *Edda* also makes mention of this flood: according to it, all the *Rimthussars* were drowned by it with the exception of the *old one on the mountain* (Berggembler).

The Mosaic record of the deluge and of Noah's ark, is too well known by us to require to be repeated. It accords in several particulars with the accounts of other oriental nations, and of the time recorded by them, namely, from 2500 to 3000 years before Christ. The *main fact,* that a great deluge overflowed the earth, from which only a few persons were saved, is therefore *confirmed by the early traditions of all ancient nations.**

* But whence arises this unusual accordance in the account of so remote an event? *Moses,* who lived 800 years after the deluge (according to the Hebrew text of the sacred Scriptures, 650 years according to the Samaritan version, and according to the Septuagint, 1550 years), could not have obtained any other knowledge of this occurrence than that which he probably acquired by means of some document; at least the sacred Scriptures do not mention any revelation in this respect. But whence did *Moses* obtain this document? This is a question which deserves investigation.

The wonderful birth and education of *Moses* is well known: protected by the daughter of the Egyptian king, brought up in the royal palace, which was the centre of the pomp of a great kingdom, he was instructed in all the wisdom of the Egyptians, and thus became a man, " mighty in word and deeds." *Strabo* mentions Moses as an Egyptian priest, who endeavoured to *abolish animal sacrifices.*

Justin regards Moses as being endowed by nature with the

Having seen how the *traditions* of the most ancient nations bear witness that a great *flood* over-

most extraordinary talents, and, like his ancestor Joseph, being able to interpret dreams, and to perform miracles.

Manetho passes a less favourable judgment on Moses and his people; he calls them a miserable nation, doomed to the most contemptible and laborious work, namely, the digging of canals and making of roads; and who, in order to escape from a disgraceful slavery, chose for their leader a priest of Heliopolis, named *Osarsiph*, who gave them a new religion, and assumed the name of Moses.

Diodorus of Sicily speaks of the lawgiver of the Hebrews as a man of great wisdom and tried courage, the chief of a strange people, who lived in slavery; and who conducted them from Egypt to the neighbouring wilderness, where he gave laws, appointed priests and other officers, but retained himself the highest power, of which, from his character and intelligence, he was worthy.

Clemens of Alexandria affirms that Moses, when he attained a sufficient age, studied in the colleges of the priests in Egypt, and afterwards with the most distinguished teachers, arithmetic, geometry, rhythm, harmony, medicine, and music; moreover, that Moses had devoted his time to that kind of science which consisted in symbols and hieroglyphics, and which, by *Justin Martyr*, is denominated the symbolical part of the sacred scripture of the Egyptians.

The same *Justin Martyr* proposes the following question:—"Why Moses, who was instructed in all the sciences which then flourished in Egypt, did not also apply himself to astronomy, geometry, astrology, and such like studies?" To this question he gives the following answer:—"Moses devoted himself only to the highest science, since astronomy, astrology, and geometry were not particularly esteemed by the Egyptians. On the contrary, they set a high value upon the knowledge of hieroglyphics,

flowed the earth, and destroyed the greater part of mankind, we must now inquire how far *science* accords with *tradition*.

The father of *geological* science in its present form, *Cuvier*, expresses the following opinion, in his *Discours sur les Révolutions de la Surface du Globe*,* page 283 of the 5th Paris edition,:†—"I (*Cuvier*) consider, with Messrs. *Deluc* and *Dolomieu*, that if there is anything established in geology, it is the fact that the surface of the earth has been the subject of a great and sudden revolution, the date of which cannot go much

in which the most distinguished persons received instruction in the temples." According to another Egyptian tradition, Moses received a royal education, was at the same time formed for a prophet, legislator, warrior, statesman, and philosopher,—all of which qualities, according to the view of the ancients, were necessary for a king.

If we reflect upon all these testimonies respecting Moses (derived entirely from profane authors), and consider the *place* (Heliopolis) where he studied, and if we also recollect that the religion of the Egyptians was derived from India, we thus find a clue *from whence* Moses must partly have obtained his *cosmogony*, and also his religious system, which, like the *Vedas* was constructed upon *monotheistic* principles.

* This is, in fact, only the preface to his large work, Sur les Ossemens Fossiles.

† Vide Conclusion Générale relative à l'Epoque de la dernière Révolution.

further back than *five or six* thousand years;* that this revolution has *sunk* (enfoncé) or caused to disappear (fait disparaitre) those lands which were formerly inhabited by man, together with those species of animals which are now the most common; that, on the other hand, it has made dry (mis à sec) the former bottom of the sea, and formed of the same the lands which are now inhabited; that it was only after this revolution that the small number of individuals who were saved, spread and propagated themselves upon the ground (terrain), which then came into view; and, consequently, that it is only from this period that societies of men have existed, formed settlements, erected monuments, collected natural facts, and combined them into scientific systems.†

Although we must regard conclusions at which so eminent a man as *Cuvier* has arrived as proved,

* Cuvier's calculation respecting the period of the deluge agrees pretty nearly with the records of this event (see p. 172). *Forchhammer* says, in his Geology of Bornholm, that the Rullsten-deluge must have taken place between four and five thousand years back, thus, also, somewhat in accordance with the traditions.

† The translation is *literal,* in order that the meaning of the author might not be *misrepresented.*

when they rest upon *facts,* an *hypothesis* set up by him is not of so *binding* a nature. I admit, with *Cuvier,* " that the surface of the earth has been the *subject of a great and sudden revolution,* the date of which cannot go much farther back than *five* or *six* thousand years," but I question the very possibility " that this revolution has sunk (enfoncé) or caused to disappear all those lands which were then inhabited by man; made dry the former bottom of the sea, and formed of this, the land which is now inhabited."

My doubts rest upon the following grounds:—

1. Neither *Cuvier, Deluc,* nor *Dolomieu* has adduced a single *fact* or a single *reason* in support of this point.

2. It calls to mind Plato's account of the disappearing of *Atlantis* (Vide the Timæus, and Critias of Plato), which *Cuvier* himself calls *Romanesque,* p. 192.

3. " If all those lands which were formerly inhabited by man, together with those kinds of animals which are now most common, should have sunk (enfoncé), or have disappeared, whilst the present continents had raised themselves from

the bottom of the sea;" how could, in such a case, a single human being, or a single animal, have escaped from those parts of the world, which *were entirely sunk?*

4. The records of all ancient nations, indicate plainly, many of the countries which were overflowed by the deluge, such as China, India, Persia, Chaldea, Babylon, Armenia, Greece, &c. Accounts which could not have existed, if the parts of the world which were overflowed had, according to *Cuvier*, sunk to the bottom of the sea.

These reasons induce me to regard the hypothesis set up by *Cuvier*, *Deluc*, and *Dolomieu*, as improbable, and not based upon *geological facts;* on the contrary, it appears probable *that the last great deluge* overflowed the present parts of the world*, and not a continent sunk to the bottom of the sea.

Did this deluge overflow different parts of the earth *successively*, or the whole planet *at once?* Were the *Noachidæ* alone saved, or

* The *geological* inundations which happened in primitive times, cannot here come in question, but only the *historical* deluge.

other persons also? To these questions *geology* affords no decisive answer.

Let us now see what information *geology* supplies respecting another important question, namely, Whether *man* was created or not, when the great deluge took place? *Cuvier* expresses himself on this point in the following manner (see the same work, page 351) :—

"What is most astonishing is the fact, that among all those *mammifera,* of which the greater part now have their species (congeneres) in the *warm climates,* there is not found a single *quadrumane,* not a single bone or tooth of any *monkey;* not even a bone or a tooth of an extinct species. Neither has there been found (in *diluvial strata*) any human being; all the bones of our species which have been discovered, together with the fossil remains of the animals, of which we (Cuvier) have spoken, have been found *accidentally* there, and their number is small, which certainly would not have been the case if *men* had made settlements in the lands which were inhabited by these animals.

"*But where, then, was the human race?*" exclaims *Cuvier,*—"this most perfect work of the Creator? Did it exist anywhere upon the earth? Those kinds of animals by which men are now surrounded, and of which no remains are found among the *fossils,* did they surround them then? The country which they together inhabited, has it been sunk (engloutis), whilst the lands which are now inhabited have again come into view (ont été remis à sec)? Respecting all these questions, the study of *fossils* affords no information, and we must not here have recourse to other sources than these."

Cuvier appears thus to doubt the *existence of man* on those parts of the earth which are now brought in view (mis à sec), at the time when the great deluge occurred (see page 137); however, he thus expresses himself in page 138:—

"I will not thence conclude that man could not have existed *before* this period, since he might possibly have inhabited some smaller country, from which, after these terrible events, he might again be able to people the earth."

But if the before-mentioned *hypothesis* of *Cuvier* be true, namely, that all the countries then existing were sunk into the bottom of the sea, how could man have been saved from the general destruction "in some smaller country?"

Other distinguished geologists do not go so far as Cuvier. Thus Buckland, for instance (in his excellent work 'Geology and Mineralogy considered with reference to Natural Theology,' page 103), says, that not a trace of man has been found *in the series of the geological formations.* Lyell expresses himself in a similar manner. (See 'Principles of Geology,' Vol. I. page 153.)

Thus we find that whilst Cuvier maintains that man did not exist upon the earth (at least not in any of the present continents) at the time of the last great deluge, Buckland and Lyell only say that no human being has been found in the *series of those geological formations*, which, according to their system, comprise the periods of the tertial series, *Eocena, Miocena,* and *Pliocena.*

For the last of these periods, Buckland, in his remarkable work, *Reliquiæ Diluvianæ,* has specified the kinds of animals which then existed, among the fossil bones of which no human bone has been discovered. *Buckland* declares, however, that he does not consider this flood *identical* with that recorded in the sacred scriptures.

Forchhammer asserts, in his *geological* lectures, " that petrified human bones have been found from the *diluvial period*, and that the human race actually existed before the cataclysm we call the deluge, and survived it.

Von Schlottheim states that he discovered *human bones* in a fissure of a rock at Costritz, together with fossils of the rhinoceros (consequently a Pachyderma of the tertial period).

Christol, Marcel de Serres,* and Boué have discovered a great number of human bones and skulls, together with fossils of tropical animals, in grottoes in the south of France.†

Buckland states, in the above-mentioned work, *Reliquæ Diluvianæ*, that he found the skeleton of a woman, together with needles of bone, in a grotto at *Pavyland*.‡

Cuvier says that he found the jaw-bone of a man at *Nica*, but cannot tell at what period it came there.

* Marcel de Serres, Journal de Géologie, T. III. page 245.

† Annales des Sciences Naturelles, T. XII. page 78; T. XVIII. page 242.

‡ The human skeleton found in *Guadaloupe* is *not fossil*, it is from a very recent period, the time of the discovery of the island by the Spaniards.

Schmerling expresses his conviction that the human bones which were found in the grottoes at Liège are contemporaneous with the fossils by which they were surrounded (see Recherches sur les Ossemens Fossiles des Cavernes de Liège); and Silliman (the most remarkable instance) says, that in North America petrified human bones have been found, together with fossils of the *mastodon,* not only in grottoes and clefts of rocks, but in *diluvial strata.* (See 'American Journal,' Vol. XXXVI. page 198.)

Without entering into an examination of these different statements, we may admit the following conclusions, namely:—

1st. That the existence of man upon the earth is *more recent* than the series of the geological formations to which the Miocena period of the tertial formations, if not also its Pliocena, must be reckoned.

2nd. That the existence of man upon the earth is older than the last great deluge, as is demonstrated by *scripture, history,* and *geology.*

3rd. That the existence of man upon the earth must consequently have taken place *between these two periods,* which probably were separated from each other by many thousand years.

4th. That, therefore, human bones might be found together with fossils of *antediluvian* animals, but not with those of animals of those kinds which belong to the period of the geological formations.

It does not appear to agree either with the statements of the sacred scripture, or with history, or with geology, that the human race, with the exception of the *Noachidæ,* has been extirpated by that cataclysm, since the scripture makes mention of the cities of *Babel* and *Nineveh* (Gen. x. 8-11; xi. 1-7), already in the third generation of Noah, the building and peopling of which, though never so small, could not possibly have been accomplished in the short space of three generations, if there were no other men upon the earth than the posterity of the eight persons who were saved. The olive-leaf brought by the dove also proves that the flood did not reach the heights on which the olive-tree grows, because the latter, in this case, in the long space of one hundred and fifty days during which the deluge prevailed, must necessarily have been destroyed. Thus, men might also have saved themselves upon heights which were not reached by the flood.

Since, then, the Mosaic narrative appears to admit the possibility of other persons besides the *Noachidæ,* having saved themselves from the great deluge, and since the traditions of all ancient nations testify that such was the case, and even record the *names* of the individuals saved, we are justified in assuming *that the Noachidæ were not the only persons upon the earth, who were preserved from the great deluge.*

If, with the sacred scriptures, we recognize a *common father* of the human race, we must also admit a *common point of departure* from which the race proceeded.

Upon what part of the earth this point was situated, is a question which we must now examine. In this, as well as in all other respects, we must first consult our own sacred records, and it is only when these are silent, or express themselves indefinitely, that we are allowed to seek other sources for the solution of the question.

At the time when Moses wrote, according to the biblical computations, upwards of 4000 years had elapsed *from the creation of the first man.** Moses, therefore, could know no more of the locality in which the first man was found, than we ourselves know, unless by means of *revelation.* Such a revelation is not mentioned in the Mosaic narrative, and if it had been afforded, it would probably have been geographically more comprehensible, than what is recorded in the book of Genesis respecting the four rivers.

We make this statement merely to show that the Mosaic account offers no obstacle to our endeavouring to ascertain the *locality* in which mankind first dwelt.

By this locality I do not mean (as has been

* J. Müller adopts the following computation after the *Alexandrine* text of the Mosaic books. See Versuch über die Zeitrechnungen der Vorwelt :—

	Years.
From the beginning to the flood (according to Julius Africanus)	2262
To the first-born of Terah	1072
To the birth of Abraham (according to Usher)	60
To Abraham's expatriation	75
To the going down into Egypt	212
To the departure from Egypt	430
Total	4111 years.

already stated), the *biblical Eden,* but the locality where mankind, already united to a people, first resided, perhaps *thousands of years* after the creation of man, yet at a period far preceding the cataclysm called the deluge.*

* The distinguished orientalist, Professor Rask, of Copenhagen, in a pamphlet published in 1828, on '*The most Ancient Hebrew Chronology until Moses,*' has made a comparison between the age of the *Adamites,* according to biblical years, and their age according to solar years. According to this calculation not more than 713 years elapsed between *Adam* and *Noah.*

Rask thence draws the conclusion, which is confirmed by many biblical citations, "*that Adam was not the first man upon the earth, consequently not the father of the whole human race,*" although he certainly might be the first man within the localities comprised in the Mosaic writings, and thus the father of the human race which proceeded from these localities, and called the *Caucasian,* from which the Europeans for the most part are descended.

Without entering upon an examination of this view, it seems, however, *probable* that man's first existence upon the earth must be earlier than 713 years before Noah, which would not be more than 3200 years before Christ (according to another calculation of Rask, not more than 2700 years before Christ) which is much too short a period, compared with that testified by the traditions of all the other ancient nations, and especially when compared with the age of the great pyramid at *Gizeh* (see page 42), as confirmed by astronomical calculations, which is 5000 years earlier than the birth of Christ, and consequently 2000 years older than the period maintained as that of the existence of the first man upon the earth.

The very exact position of this pyramid (as of all the rest) to

In order to ascertain this locality we shall commence our inquiry with the remarkable record of the Zend people, called *Zend-Avesta* which has been already referred to.

In the first chapter (*Fargard*) of the part, which bears the name *Vendidad, Ormuzd* (the good principle, in opposition to *Ahriman*, the evil principle), expresses himself to *Zapetman* (Zoroaster) in the following terms :—

"I have given to man an excellent and fertile country; nobody is able to give such a one.* In

the four cardinal points, which could not be better accomplished at the present day with the aid of the most perfect mathematical and astronomical instruments, proves, moreover, that the Egyptians, at this remote period, were already in a very advanced state of culture, which again presupposes a lapse of thousands of years for its attainment; accordingly, we cannot conceal from ourselves that the existence of man upon the earth must be of a far higher date than that which is indicated by the Mosaic chronology.

* I here follow the translation of the Zend-Avesta, by Anquetil du Perron, which appears to me to be the best.

Heeren, in his excellent work, ' Ideen über die Politik und den Handel der alten Völker," made use of another translation (Kleuker's), which appears to me to be so far incorrect inasmuch as it states that the country which Ormuzd had bestowed upon man, had changed its climate from a winter of five months into one of ten months, a physical impossibility not contained in the Zend-Avesta.

Burnouf dit, dans ses Commentaires sur le Yacna, que la

this land the winter lasts, *in certain regions, ten months,* in other parts not more than *five* months of the year; in those the summer lasts *seven* months. The winter is severe; the water freezes, but this is a blessing; for after the cold everything grows magnificently. This land lies to the east (of Persia), lies where the stars rise every evening."

"When Djemshid (the leader of the emigrating nation) came from the high land in the east, to the plain, there were neither domestic animals, nor wild, nor men."

Those passages are remarkable on several accounts; they prove—

1. That the country from which Djemschid came was an elevated mountain-land, where the winter, "*in certain regions*" (upon the high mountains), lasted ten months (as on the Alps), and

traduction d'*Anquetil* n'est point juste, et que l'original Zend, du Zend-Aveste, dit que Djemshid est venu du *nord*, et non de *l'est;* mais comment concilier cette version avec ce que dit le Zend-Aveste, que Djemshid est venu du pays où l'on voit chaque soir (en Sogdiane) les *étoiles se lever;* cela ne peut-être que l'est.

Mais admettons même que Djemshid soit arrivé en Sogdiana du *nord*, et non de *l'est*, où cela nous conduit-il? c'est encore vers la Chaine de l'*Altai* et le haut plateau de l'Asie centrale.

where, "*in other parts*" (the low lands) it did not last more than five months.

2. That the country from which Djemschid came, was situated to the east of the land where the *Zend-Avesta* was composed (that is to say, in the east of Persia);* *that the stars rose there every evening*; thus a proof that the land lay in the east, and could not be Mesopotamia, Armenia, or any of the countries probably indicated in the Mosaic records, all of which were to the west of Persia.

3. That the country to which Djemschid came was desolate and uninhabited; that neither men, tame nor wild beasts were found there.

4. That the country from which Djemschid came was situated between 36 and 48 degrees of latitude, where the proportion stated between the length of the summer and winter takes place.

All these statements point to the *high land of Central Asia*,† with its mountain plateaus, where

* Zoroaster, the author of the Zend-Avesta, was born, and wrote in the town of *Orumia* (*Ooroomis*) not far from *Tabur*, in the most western part of Persia, on the borders of Armenia.

† The best description of the *high land of Central Asia*,

the winter lasts ten months, and its low lands, where it lasts but five months, a country situated to the east of Persia, and not the *west*.

is given by *Alexander von Humboldt*, in his excellent work entitled *Asie Centrale.* Vide p. 5, Paris edition of 1843. " Un plateau d'une hauteur considerable s'étend très probablement sans interruption, dans la direction du sud-sud-ouest au nord-nord-est, depuis la petite Boukharie jusqu'aux Khalkas orientaux et à la chaine du Khangkai. En s'appuyant sur les positions astronomiques de Khotau et de Peking, déterminées par le Père Hallerstein et M. George Tuss, on trouve que le plateau mentioné est compris entre les méridiens de 79° et 116°, et que les bords les plus méridienaux et le plus septentrionaux se trouvent par les 36° et 48° de latitude, ce que, par les sinuosités du désert, qui n'est aucunement dépourvu de pâturages et de végétation, donne au plateau du Cha-mo du Gobi de quarante-deux à quarante-trois mille lieues carrées marines. En ajoutant à cette étendue du Gobi le haut plateau du Tubet qui en est séparé par la grande chaine des montagnes du Kouenloun au Koulkoun, on aura, d'après mes calculs, depuis la pente septentrionale de l'Himalaya jusqu'au Khangkai de la Mongolie Chinoise, c'est à dire, depuis le lac de Manasa et le Kaylas Tubetain, jusqu'à la limite nord-est du Gobi, une longueur transversale de 520 lieues au une surface renflée de soixante à soixante-deux mille lieues carrées; c'est, à peu près quatre fois la surface de la France, c'est une aire, à peine plus considerable que celle qu'occupa, sous l'aspect d'une longue bande, le massif soulevé de la Cordillére des Andes dans l'Amérique méridionale. Je compare ici deux genres de soulèvements très différents par leur forme et leur âge rélatif. En Asie l'axe du grand plateau est dirigé du sud-ouest au nord-est, et son existence est certainement antérieure aux grandes chaines de montagnes dont nous allons tracer le tableau dans cet ouvrage,

In the second chapter of the Zend-Avesta, Ormuzd expresses himself in the following manner: —

"The second blessed place, which I, who am Ormuzd, presented to mankind, was *Soghdi* (Sogdiana); the third was *Bakhdi* (Bactria); the fourth was *Nesa* (a region in Khorassan, which still bears the same name); and the fifth was *Ver* (Fars, Farsistan)."

et que elles-mêmes se prolongent dans le sens des parallèles à l'équateur.

En restreignant le nom de plateau d'Asie à la zone que je viens de circonscrire d'après l'ensemble de nos connaissances actuelles, il faut se hâter d'ajouter que cette zone, bien loin de remplir l'immense espace de l'Asie intérieure, offre cependant comparativement, la plus grande *continuité* d'un exhaussement du sol en plateaux que l'on ait trouvé dans les divers continents. Quant à sa hauteur absolue au dessus du niveau de l'ocean, elle est encore aujourd'hui aussi incertaine que l'étoit jadis son extension horizontale: nous ne connoissons cette hauteur que vers ses extrémités au nord et au sud.

Page 11. En franchissant la chaine du Kouenloun vers le sud, nous arrivons à ce vaste et célèbre soulèvement du sol que remplit l'espace entre le Kouenloun et l'Himalaya.

Page 13. Si l'on examine avec attention l'ensemble des rapports que nous possédons, et si l'on compare ces rapports avec les descriptions minutieuses faites sur les lieux par des auteurs Chinois, on reconnait que le plateau *Tubetain*, loin d'être contenu, se trouve souvent interrompu, surtout dans sa partie orientale par des groupes et chainons de montagne qui le parcourent en différentes situations.

But does not this also prove, that mankind came from the east of Persia (namely, from the high land of Central Asia), and proceeded more and more to the *westward?*

Had man's first abode been in Mesopotamia, Armenia, or in the vicinity of the Euphrates,* the immigration into Persia would have been *from the west,* and in this case, a book written there, could not have stated that the first inhabitants came from the *east.*

Having examined the records of the *Zend nations,* we must now pass on to those of the *Chinese.*

According to what has been already mentioned, the *historical* records of China do not go further back than the reign of *Schihoang*, 250 years before Christ; but their *traditions* extend as far as the reign of *Fohi,* 3000 years before Christ.

According to these traditions, noted in the Schu-king, the ancestors of the Chinese, conducted by *Fohi,* came to the plains of China 2900 years before Christ, *from the high mountain-land which lies*

* *Phrat* has been considered to denote the *Euphrates,* but the word signifies *river in general,* and not the *Euphrates* in particular.

to the west of that country,—that is to say, from the high land of Central Asia. The very locality from which the immigration took place is stated in the *Schuking*, namely, the vicinity of the *Baikal lake*, which by the people of Central Asia, and their neighbours in Siberia, is still called the *sacred lake*.* According to the records of the Schuking, the Chinese nation is then derived from the *high land of Central Asia*.

Let us now pass on to the documents of the *Hindoos*, in order to ascertain the primitive abode of the fathers of this race.

The most ancient writings of the Hindoos agree that the Brahmin and the Khetry castes, came *from the north* to India, from a *high mountain land*, which in seven steps raises itself from the plains of India up to the North Pole, where *Skand*, the god of war, reigns. The *high land of Central Asia* corresponds to this description. The seven steps consist of the double chain of the *Himalaya*,

* It is a curious fact, that it was from the shores of the same lake that *Dschingis Khan*, 3000 years after *Fohi*, went to conquer China from the descendants of *Fohi*. He extended his conquests afterwards from China to India, and so far in the west as to Bohemia, founding the greatest empire which has ever been seen on earth.

the *Kokonorian* chain, the double *Karakumenian* chain, the *Kouenloun,* and the *Altai* chain, forming together what are figuratively called the seven steps.

The Mahab-harata, and the Ramajana celebrate the arrival of the Brahmin and Khetry castes from the high land situated to the north of India, and their conquest of this country, then probably inhabited only by *settlers,* who in former times came to clear the forests, and their descendants (so as the west of America is inhabited by descendants of settlers coming from the eastern provinces).

Such probably has been the case in India. First came some few emigrants from the high neighbouring land; others followed, until finally the great immigration took place, which, under the name of a conquest, is celebrated in the epic poems of the Hindoos.

We have now seen the coincident statements of three of the most ancient nations of Asia: the Persians, the Chinese, and the Hindoos, that their ancestors came from the *high land of Central Asia;* and as these statements have every appearance of probability, and we cannot expect more definite information from times so remote, those statements may be considered as *historically established.**

They all testify that the progenitors of the human race, during a certain period, the length of which cannot be calculated, dwelt on the high land of Central Asia, probably *at that time united in one nation*, whose language was the ancient *Pelvi*, from which the *Sanscrit*, the *Zend*, and the *Kouwen* are derivations, languages which now constitute the tongues of the three nations who emigrated from the central land, namely, the *Hindoos*, the *Persians*, and the *Chinese*.†

* Joh. von Müller expresses himself in the following manner in his Allgemeine Geschichte, Band I. p. 25. In order to ascertain the country in which the human race first dwelt, no method appears to me to be more certain than that of inquiring where *bread*, the universal staff of life, and those *domestic animals* which are most generally useful, were indigenous; for it is probable that man on his first immigration took with him his usual means of support, and those animals which had accompanied him in his domestic life. Theophrastus observes, that corn grows wild in the mountain lands on the other side of the Caspian Sea. A pupil of Linné (Heinzelmann) found corn growing wild in Baschkiria. Thus much is certain, that in the mountain land of Cashmeer, in Tibet, and in the north of China, it grows for several years without sowing or cultivation, and also that our *domestic animals* run about wild in the mountainous tracts of these countries.

† In China there are properly *four* languages or develop-

How far this primitive people possessed that high degree of civilization which Bailly and some others attribute to it, is a question which, if not credible, nevertheless deserves examination. The reasons assigned for this high degree of civilization rest principally upon the opinion of Bailly.*

1. That the astronomy of the Hindoos, of the Chinese, and of the Chaldeans, appears to be rather "*the remains, than the elements of a science*" (plutôt les débris que les élémens d'une science), and consequently presupposes a very ancient nation, from whom the *science* is derived, which forms the germ of these remains.

2. That the Hindoos, the Persians, the Egyptians, and the Chinese, from the earliest periods of their history, divided the time *alike*, namely,

ments of the original language *Kou-wen.* The most ancient records are written in this language, which at the present time is understood by none but the most learned Mandarins. It is allied to the *Sanscrit.* The second is called *Wontschang,* and forms the epic language; the third is called *Kuanhoa,* and is the language of the Mandarins (being derived from the *Kou-wen*); the fourth is the common language of the people, called *Kiang-tang,* together with different dialects for each of the different provinces of the empire.

* See his Histoire de l'Astronomie Ancienne.

the year into 12 months, and 365¼ days, and the day into 24 hours; that they divided the *Zodiac alike,* into twelve signs; that they divided the *week alike,* into seven days, which, being an *arbitrary* division, could not be the result of *accident,* but proves that they obtained it from the common source of an *ancient people,* who already possessed a high degree of astronomical science, and consequently a high degree of *civilization.*

Let us now examine these reasons of *Bailly.* If we admit a *common father* of the whole family of mankind, we must admit a primitive nation. That this nation, during a certain period, dwelt on the high land of Central Asia, appears to be confirmed by the traditions of the Hindoos, the Chinese, and the Persians; but that this people had attained *a high degree of civilization,* is contradicted by these very traditions. The *Vedas* represents the religion of the ancient people as a *Sabeism,* or worship of the sun and stars, which proves that this people was in a primitive state of development. The Chinese speak of *Fohi,* their first leader from the high land, as a *shepherd,* leading a nomadic life; and the Persians speak of *Djemschid* in the same way, which precludes a high degree of civilization.*

On the other hand, tradition proves that Brahmaism developed itself on the shores of the *Ganges*, the *Jumna,* and the *Nerbudda,* the sacred rivers in whose waves alone, the Brahmin can wash away his sins and attain *Nirvani.*

It is *there* we must seek not alone for the cradle of the Brahmin religion, but for the cradle of the high civilization of the Hindoos, which gradually extended itself in the west to *Ethiopia,* to *Egypt,* and to *Phœnicia ;* in the east to *Siam,* to *China,* and to *Japan ;* in the south to *Ceylon,* to *Java,* and to *Sumatra ;* and in the north to *Persia,* to *Chaldea,* and to *Colchis,* whence it came to *Greece* and to *Rome,* and at length to the remote abodes of the *Hyperboreans.*

If, therefore, we admit with *Bailly,* that there was a primitive nation (which possibly during a

* Lorsque dans le silence de l'histoire positive, guidé par l'étude féconde des langues, on veut remonter hors de la Chine, aux germes d'une antique civilization Asiatique, on n'arrive *point à ces Plateaux inhospitaliers du Nord,* on arrive à l'origine commune des deux grandes branches de la famille des peuples *Indo-persans,* aux rapports des Ariens Brahmaniques, et des Ariens Bactrians. Vide Alex. von Humboldt, Asie Centrale, Vol. I. p. 24.

certain period inhabited *Siberia**), we cannot admit that this nation possessed a high degree of *civilization*, a fact contradicted by the traditions of all ancient nations.

* See Lettre sur *l'Atlantide de Platon* à M. de Voltaire, full of the most singular trifling for so great an astronomer as Bailly.

Bailly has made a comparison between the Hindoo names of the seven days of the week, and their names among the *Egyptians* and the *Romo-Grecian* nations (Astronomie Indienne, page 6 of the Paris edition, 4to.). I will attempt a comparison between the Hindoo names of the days of the week and those of the Scandinavians.

Sunday is called by the Hindoos *Additavaram*, from *Additia*, the *sun*. It is named from the *sun* by the Scandinavians (*Söndag*).

Monday is called *Somavaram*, from *Soma*, the *moon*. So among the Scandinavians (*Monday*).

Tuesday is called by the Hindoos *Mangelavaram*, from their hero *Mangala*. It bears its name among the Scandinavians from their hero *This* (*Tisdag*).

Wednesday is termed *Boutavaram* by the Hindoos, after *Boudha;* as by the Scandinavians it is denominated after *Oden* (Wodan, Bodhan, Budha), (*Onsdag*).

Thursday is called *Brahaspativaram* by the Hindoos, after *Brahma*, their principal god; it bears its name among the Scandinavians after their principal god *Thor* (*Thorsdag*).

Friday is called by the Hindoos *Sucravaram*, after *Sucra*, the goddess of *beauty;* it is named by the Scandinavians after *Freja*, the goddess of beauty (*Frejdag*).

Saturday is called *Sanyvaram* by the Hindoos, after *Sanyvar*, the god who cleansed spiritually. It is named by the Scandinavians *Lördag*, derived from *loger*, bathing.

We have here another proof that the myths of the Scandinavians are derived from those of the Hindoos.

THE FIRST MIGRATION UPON EARTH.

We have indicated in the last chapter, a period in which the human race was, in all probability, associated on the high land of Central Asia. We shall now inquire how far this abode has been the *first* where the human race was established, or whether there are grounds to conjecture that, previous to this period, *some other part of the earth* was inhabited by the parents of the human race.

That the Eden of the Bible is not meant by this *part of the earth*, has already been stated.

In order to enter upon this inquiry, it will be necessary to go back into the history of the formation of the earth.

The greatest authorities among the geologists all assume that there has been a period in the history of our planet, in which this planet, if not entirely, was at least on its surface, *in a fluid state*, which, according to certain geologists, has been brought about by the action of *water;* according to others, by that of *fire;* and again, according to others, by both of these *agents* united.

Fire is, however, the *agent* which appears to be most generally admitted, and seems to possess the strongest claims.*

The once *fluid* state of the earth's surface, is attested not only by a multitude of geological facts, but also by the *form* of the globe itself, being flattened at the poles.

* *Cuvier* expresses himself in the following terms on this subject (See his *Discours sur les Révolutions de la surface du Globe.* 5th Paris ed. p. 21).

" Le granit, dont les crêtes centrales de la plupart des grandes chaines de montagne sont composées, le granit qui dépasse tout, est aussi la pierre qui s'enfonce sous toutes les autres, c'est la plus ancienne de celles qu'il nous ait été donné de voir dans la place que lui assigna la nature, soit qu'elle doive son origine *à un liquid général qui, auparavant, aurait tout tenu en dissolution, soit qu'elle ait été la premiere fixée par le refroidissement d'une grande en fusion, ou même en évaporation.*

Buckland expresses himself in the following manner in his excellent work, *Geology and Mineralogy considered with reference to Natural Theology.* Lond. 1836, Vol. I. p. 39.

" We therefore commence our inquiry (of the primitive formation) at that most ancient period, when there is much evidence to render it probable *that the entire materials of the globe were in a fluid state, and that the cause of this fluidity was heat.*"

Such quotations might easily be multiplied, and, indeed, from the writings of our great naturalist, *Berzelius,* if the passages cited were not sufficient.

The *agent* which has produced this fluid state, or rather this process of fusion, must have been an *internal fire*, for the *rays of the sun*, in an atmosphere then filled with carbonic acid gas, and with the water of the sea transmuted into the form of gas, could not possess the *intensity* of heat required, to produce a fusion of the whole surface of the earth.

That the surface of the earth, at the time when this process of fusion took place, could not be inhabited by *organic beings* is evident.

Geology shows that organic beings were not created before everything on earth was ready to receive them, that is to say, not before the crust of the earth cooled to the temperature necessary for the existence of such beings.

Even under the *last period* of the geological series, this temperature was so high, that the temperature of the *polar regions, corresponded to the present temperature of the tropical regions,* which is proved by the *coal strata* found in *Nova Zembla*, by the fossil remains found in the *polar regions* from the *vegetable kingdom* (Mavritia aculeata, Palmacites Lamanonis, Elaeis Guineensis, Cocos-nucifera), which belong all to the tropical vegetation; and by the fossil remains of the animal kingdom of that period, the *Mammoth,** the *Rhinoceros,* the *Hippopotamus,* and the *Tapir,*† belonging all to tropical climates.‡

But at a time when the temperature was so high in the polar regions, how *much higher* must it not have been at the *tropics,* where the rays of the sun fall *perpendicularly,* and where the boundary of the eternal winter over our heads, by its

* Some geologists consider the woolly covering of the mammoth as a proof that this animal was destined to live in the *northern* regions. This opinion does not appear to be well founded, for the *Lama,* which is a native of *Peru,* near the equator, has an equally warm covering of wool as the mammoth, and the forepart of the *lion* has one still warmer.

† These animals were all *herbivorous ;* we may thence conclude how rich and tropical nature must have been in these polar regions to produce vegetables sufficiently succulent to support animals of so colossal a size as these. If, moreover, the tropical animals could *live* in the polar regions, still they could not *propagate* themselves, had not the climate been similar to a tropical one.

‡ Vide Remains in Tertiary Strata, *Buckland,* Vol II. p. 15. Cuvier expresses himself in the following terms respecting the animals of the tertial period, in his *Discours sur les Révolutions du Globe,* page 33. " Des carnassiers de la taille du lion, du tigre, de l'hyène, désolaient ce nouveau règne animal. En général son caractère, même dans *l'extrême nord et sur les bords de la mer glaciale d'aujourd'hui* resemblait à celui que *la seule zone torride nous offre maintenant,* et toutefois aucune espèce n'y était absolument la même."

greater distance, contributes less to the cooling of the air than at the poles; it must have been *so high, that man's physical power could not endure it.*

It is true that the fossil remains both of the animal and vegetable kingdoms,* which have been found from times that do not belong to the series of the geological periods, indicate a temperature little exceeding that which still prevails in the climates where these animals and plants are found, and that if the appearance of man upon the earth should not be older than these animals and plants, no reason can be given why this appearance should not have taken place as well in the southern as in the northern zones of the globe. But when we consider that nothing in nature is done *suddenly*, and that the cooling of the globe must have been *successively*, and, indeed, during an immense space of time, since, according to *Fourier's* observations, the cooling of the globe from a certain degree of temperature to a lower, requires a period of 1,280,000 years, the same proportion being obtained by a sphere of a foot in diameter in a second. Thus the cooling of

* See Brongniart.

the globe from the time when the temperature of the poles was *tropical,* until the time when (according to *Brongniart*) it approached to the present, must probably have required a period of millions of years.

That this cooling continued after the series of the geological periods, is demonstrated by *Elie de Beaumont* (in his examination of *Pouillet's* inquiry respecting the temperature of the *universe,* and its influence on the temperature of the *earth*), where he proves that the temperature of the surface of the earth, under the period of the *diluvial stratum* (when the mastodon lived) was several degrees higher than at present.* The appearance of man upon the earth may, therefore, have taken place at any point of time whatsoever, nearer to, or more remote from the geological

* That man lived contemporary with the Mastodon is demonstrated in *Silliman's* American Journal (page 169). So many human bones have been found, together with fossils of the broad-horned stag (Cervus Eurycerus Aldrovandi), especially in the turf-moors of Ireland (see *Brewster's* Edinb. Journal of Science, 1830, No. IV. p. 301), that we can scarcely doubt the co-existence of man with this now extinct animal. Another good authority, Dr. *A. F. Link,* considers man to have been coetaneous with several now extinct animals (see *Link's Urwelt,* 2nd edition, Berlin, 1834, p. 81).

periods; yet still the position is certain, being *based upon physical circumstances*, that the polar regions must have been sooner prepared for the reception of man, than those which are situated nearer to the equator.

Now, as the Almighty, in his supreme wisdom, does nothing without an *end*, it appears to be more in accordance with this wisdom, that the appearance of man upon the earth, should take place in those parts of the globe which were prepared for his reception, than in those which millions of years later came into a state adapted for that reception.

This leads to the natural conclusion *that the polar regions must have been inhabited earlier, than any of those regions which are situated nearer to the equator.**

* After having for several years weighed this idea, namely, that the polar regions must have been inhabited by man before those situated nearer the equator, I accidentally discovered that the forgotten and obsolete *Buffon*, has expressed this opinion more than seventy years ago (see *Epoques de la Nature*), an opinion which was taken up by *Bailly*, and introduced into several of his writings.

The difference between the proofs employed by *Buffon* and *Bailly* in support of this position, compared with those here presented, arises from the discoveries which have *since* been

As, according to the nature of the thing, *both the polar regions* must have been prepared equally early for the reception of mankind, it is *possible* that the appearance of man took place *at the same time* in both regions; perhaps the *white race* in the countries about the *north pole*, and the *black race* in those about the *south pole*. A number of difficult problems might hence be solved; but be this as it may, the position is certain, that the polar regions (each of which probably then formed a great continent) are those parts of the earth in which, according to physical grounds, man must first have appeared.

In proportion as the earth became cooler, mankind retired from the polar regions and approached to those of the tropics, whose heat had then subsided to a temperature suited to the nature of man. It is in this way that men having left their *primitive* abodes (*Siberia, Greenland, North America*, &c.), gradually penetrated nearer to the equator.

*Siberia,** which, according to this theory, was

made in geology, and in other physical sciences accessible now, but not then.

* *Olaus Rudbeck* has, from *etymological* grounds, always very

the first *in our* Asiatic-European continent,* to receive mankind, was not then, as now, desolate and cold. No! it was a country where the palm-tree raised its rich crown, where the hippopotamus bathed in the rivers, and where the mammoth rejoiced in the luxurious vegetation of the tropics. It was the land of the golden age, the mythic eras, and the Hyperborean culture, spoken of by *Plato* and *Solon*, by the *Vedas of India*, and by the Egyptian priests of *Sais!*

But in proportion as the temperature of the earth decreased, this land lost its tropical climate; then our ancestors left it for more southern countries, and following in their migration the river-valleys (*Obi, Jenisei, Irtish, Lena*,†) *i. e.* came to

uncertain, endeavoured to prove (in his *Atlantica*) that the first abode of man was in Scandinavia, which he considered to be the same country as the *Atlantis of Plato*. This hypothesis, chimerical in itself, has received a further refutation from *Buch*, *Berzelius*, and *Lyell*, who have proved that the Scandinavian peninsular hill rises from the sea, and probably was situated *below the sea* at the remote period in question.

* *Asia* and *Europe* are connected together, and do not form more than *one* continent.

† It is along those rivers that the great number of fossil remains have been found of those animals which might be of service to the first, and probably *nomadic*, race of men in their migrations, such as the *primitive-horse* (which is still found in the

the *high land of Central Asia, where these rivers take their rise;* it is *there* we have found them in a period of thousands of years subsequently.

That the human race in the beginning must have had another abode than the high lands of Central Asia, is rendered still more probable from the consideration that man, in his primitive, naked, and helpless state, not to become a prey to the severity of the seasons, required *an even and mild temperature*, such, for instance, as is found on the high mountain-plateaus of South America (*Quito, Pastos, Titicaca*, &c.), where the thermometer, during the whole year, stands at from 60° to 70° Fahrenheit, and where a *continual summer* yields a constant supply of the necessaries of life.

But such a climate is not to be found in the high land of Central Asia, " where the winter, in the lowest situations, lasts *five*, and in the highest, *ten* months."

The *polar regions* must, during the time when the earth's *internal fire* affected its then *thinner*

deserts of *Cobi*), the *buffalo-ox*, and the *mammoth*, which possibly at that period supplied the place of the *camel*.

surface, more than now have had an *even* and *temperate* climate, independent of the changes of the seasons, and more suited to the *helpless* and *naked* condition of the first men, than that which prevailed then on the high land of Central Asia.

The great river-valleys of Siberia must, according to this hypothesis, as we have seen, lead our ancestors *up* to the high land of Central Asia where these rivers have their source, it is alike natural that other river-valleys would conduct them *down* to the adjacent countries. Thus the *Oxus* and *Jaxartes* (*Gihon* and *Sihon*) would lead them to *Sogdiana* and *Bactria* (as the *Zend-Avesta* has shown) the *Hoangho* and *Hoi-ho* * to the plains of *China* (as the *Schuking* has shown?) and the *Indus, Ganges,* and *Jumna,* lead them to India.†

* The *Hoangho* and *Hoi-ho* are two connected arms of the same river, namely, of that which afterwards received the common name of *Hoangho,* or the *Yellow-river.*

† According to the most recent voyages of discovery, the *Oxus* takes its rise in the lake *Sir-i-Kol,* on the *Pamenian* table land, 17,667 feet above the level of the sea, according to *Alex. von Humboldt,* but 19,000 feet according to *John Wood,* in his Narrative of a Journey to the Sources of the River *Oxus,* page 354. The *Jaxartes* has its source in the great chain of mountains, *Tian-okan,* which forms the southern boundary of

Thus the *river-valleys* and *water-systems* of Asia determined the *course of human migrations*, and conducted mankind to those parts of the world where, according to the wisdom of the Almighty, they best might spread their species.

According to the theory here presented, our ancestors' original home, was in the *polar regions*, where natural science bears testimony thereof. From thence they migrated to the *high land of Central Asia*, where *tradition* tells us of their long abode; and from this high land they wandered down to *India*, *China*, and *Persia*, where *poesy* celebrates their arrival, and where history confirms their final settlement.

But *when* has all this taken place? demands the philosopher; it was at the beginning of the present geological period, and long before the cataclysm

the northern plateau of Central Asia; the *Hoangho* takes its rise in the Lake of Stars, called *Djuring-noor*, on the high land of Thibet; but the *Indus*, the *Sutledi*, and the *Brahmapootra* have their source in the same high land of Thibet, in the sacred lakes *Ramana-hruda* and *Manassa*, (14,000 feet above the level of the sea, according to Humboldt, and 17,000, according to Moorcroft and Tucbeck). The *Ganges and Jumna* take their rise in the Trovin Kamaus of the Himalaya mountains, 24,000 feet above the level of the sea, according to Humboldt.

we call the deluge; this *geology*, *tradition*, and *history* tells us, but nothing more.

The natural sciences have in modern times unveiled organic life, as it existed at periods preceding the creation of man, by millions of years; they have made it possible to trace, from physical grounds, the first abode and the first migrations of man; and they have in their collected results given the astonishing conclusion, *that nothing upon earth is perishable, that matter only changes its form,—is immortal, like the spirit!*

A Tabular Extract from the work of *Champollion* on Egypt.

A View of the Dynasties according to Manetho.

Succession of Dynasties.	Origin.	Number of Kings.	Period of their Reign.	Commencement before the birth of Christ.
1st	Tinite Thébaïne .	8	252	5867
2nd	Tinite Thébaïne .	9	297	5615*
3rd	Memphite . . .	8	197	5318
4th	Memphite . . .	17	448	5121
5th	Eléphantine . .	9†	248*	4673
6th	Memphite . . .	6†	203	4425
7th	Memphite . . .	5	75	4222
8th	Memphite . . .	5	100	4147
9th	Héracléopolite . .	4	100	4047
10th	Héracléopolite . .	19	185	3947
11th	Thébaïne . . .	17	59	3762
12th	Thébaïne . . .	7	245	3703
13th	Thébaïne . . .	60	453	3417
14th	Xoïte	76	484	3004
15th	Thébaïne . . .	76	250	2520
16th	Thébaïne . . .	5	190	2270
17th	Thébains Pharaons.	6	260	2082
	Pasteurs . . .	6		
18th	Thébaïne . . .	17	348	1822
19th	Thébaïne . . .	6	194	1473
20th	Thébaïne . . .	12	178	1279
21st	Tanite	7	130	1101
22nd	Bubastite . . .	9†	120†	971
23rd	Tanite	4†	89†	851
24th	Saïte	1	44	762
25th	Ethiopienne . .	3	44	718
26th	Saïte	9	150†	674‡
27th	Persane . . .	8	120	524§
28th	Saïte	1	6	404
29th	Mendésienne . .	5	21	398
30th	Sébennetique . .	3	38	377
31st	Persane . . .	3	8	339
End of their government				331

* The first king of this dynasty was called *Souphi*. After a reign of 63 years, he was immediately succeeded by *Sensasouphi*, who reigned 66 years, and after him came *Manchérès*, whose reign also lasted 63 years.

† According to Julius Africanus.

‡ According to Julius Africanus, Eusebius, and the tables of kings compared with each other.

§ The conquest of Egypt by Cambyses is placed at 525 years before Christ.